Picturing
the
World

John Gilmour

STATE UNIVERSITY OF NEW YORK PRESS

To Sheila,
who made it possible

Published by
State University of New York Press, Albany

For information, address State University of New York
Press, State University Plaza, Albany, N.Y., 12246

Library of Congress Cataloging in Publication Data
Gilmour, John, 1939-
    Picturing the world.

    Bibliography: p.
    Includes index.
        1. Art—Philosophy.   2. Art, Modern—20th century.
I. Title.
N70.G55   1985   701   85-17189
ISBN 0-88706-092-7
ISBN 0-88706-093-5 (pbk.)

10   9   8   7   6   5   4   3   2   1

Contents

Illustrations

Preface

Issues raised by modern art are of interest to philosophers as well as to the art public, since they raise questions about reality, the mind, thinking, perception, and interpretation. The concerns of modern artists are strikingly similar to questions dominant in twentieth century philosophy. This study addresses those common concerns and takes a position on what philosophy has to offer to the arts and what the artist may contribute to the philosopher. The common ground between them has not always been evident to the members of either profession. One reason is that philosophical aesthetics, with its grounding in the philosopher's epistemological concerns, has often appeared inaccessible or uninteresting to the artist. In the present volume I aspire to an approach to the philosophy of art which ackowledges inspiration and instruction from particular art works, and which should be judged against the standard of the light it sheds on them and on the creative process. The artist should find the resulting analysis pertinent to his work.

Aside from this direct contribution to the literature in philosophy of art, I hope also to join those who are attempting to remove the barriers which separate the different schools of philosophy from each other. There are encouraging signs that conversations across diverse traditions may create a new vigor in American philosophy. Thinkers trained in the traditions of process philosophy, pragmatism, analytic philosophy, phenomenology, and hermeneutics have begun to master each other's idioms and address common concerns. In a modest way I wish to contribute to this development. My personal odyssey has included serious study of such diverse thinkers as Whitehead, Peirce, and Dewey; Wittgenstein, Sellars, and Rorty; Nietzsche, Heidegger, Merleau-Ponty, and Gadamer. In time this reading became focused on issues in the philosophy of mind and the philosophy of art.

The present work results from two convergent occurrences: the first was a National Endowment for Humanities Summer Seminar in the philosophy of mind in 1975, directed by Richard Rorty, which provided the intellectual focus for these studies; the second was a discussion group at Alfred University, which inspired me to apply these conceptual insights to the visual arts. Rorty's contribution to my thinking, like those of my graduate mentor Charles Hartshorne, are reflected in many pages of this work. The discussion group members provided the energy, enthusiasm, and personal support necessary for sustained thinking. Although the group had a somewhat fluid membership, several individuals were the continuing core of the group, and these individuals contributed to my ideas about art: Dan Davidson, Tom Peterson, Randy McGowan, Rick Velkley, and Dolores Iorizzo. In particular Dan Davidson deserves credit for some ideas about painting that appear in these pages, since our conversations about modern art over ten years, together with his critical reading of the manuscript, have contributed materially to what I present here. Another valued friend and colleague, Tom Peterson, deserves special credit as well. We have team-taught two seminars on subjects related to this book and he has read every version of the manuscript, contributing valuable insights and ego-support along the way.

A second NEH Summer Seminar, led by Joseph Margolis in 1980, has substantially shaped my understanding of the concept of culture. Margolis and the other members of the seminar are due my thanks, especially for strengthening my understanding of the themes of the second half of the book. Numerous people have made contributions to the final result: Carol Dunn, who edited most of the chapters; the Alfred University Research Foundation for financial support; Alfred University for a sabbatical leave; Sally Campbell, Tom Leddy, and Charles Altieri for reading and commenting on earlier versions; Richard Rorty and

Richard Bernstein for reading the manuscript and helping it along; three student assistants—Christi Scheele, Dawn Payne, and Diane Zimmerman Wall—for help with research, correspondence, and manuscript preparation; Barbara Sanford for typing the majority of the manuscript (assisted along the way by Pat Ricklefs, Diane Kelley, and Linda Hardy); Dan Harvey, Jay Hullett, and Stuart Campbell for valuable advice about publishing; Bill Wall and Sheila Wall Gilmour for help with proofreading and indexing.

Perhaps most of all I owe thanks to numerous students at Alfred University in several courses since 1978; and to my wife, Sheila Wall Gilmour, and my stepdaughter, Mary Wall, who have conversed freely and insightfully with me about themes that are central to this study. None of these people is, of course, responsible for errors and misinterpretations contained in these pages.

Acknowledgement is given, also, to the following publishers for permission to quote from sources under copyright: the editors of *Process Studies* to quote from my earlier article, "Art and the Expression of Meaning" (vol. 13, 1983, pp. 71–87); the editors of the *Journal of Philosophy* to quote from Richard Rorty's article, "The World Well Lost" (vol. 69, 1972, p. 662); to Crossroads/Continuum for quotation from Hans Georg Gadamer, *Truth and Method* (1975); Northwestern University Press for substantial quotation from Maurice Merleau-Ponty, *Signs* (1964); and Alfred Knopf for permission to quote from Wallace Stevens' "The Man with the Blue Guitar" in Stevens' *Collected Poems* (1955).

Introduction

The artist's studio and the scientist's laboratory are two of the places where work occurs. However, our spontaneous image of them is utterly different. We think of them as having radically divergent purposes, making the people who work in either setting uncomfortable in the other. Although an artist of the past like Leonardo da Vinci may have flourished in both, such breadth is unlikely in artists of the contemporary world. How are we to think of this difference between laboratory and studio, which symbolizes a breach in our world? Our almost automatic response is to give the priority to laboratory over studio, since the laboratory seems designed for more serious purposes. After all, the laboratory has an aura of serious research; the continual refinement of method gives the conscientious scientist a seemingly objective access to nature. The laboratory reflects the scientist's commitment to truth. In contrast, the artist's commitment is to creativity. Creativity and truth seem to be divergent values. What does the emphasis on creativity imply about the artist and his function in an age which gives priority to the laboratory?

A particularly compelling portrait of the artist's studio is presented by Matisse. His *The Red Studio* (Figure 1) displays an artist's studio with neither artist nor artist's model. No work is being done. Only the

Fig. 1 Henri Matisse, *The Red Studio* (1911)
Oil on canvas, 71-¼" × 7'2-¼". Mrs. Simon Guggenheim Fund Collection, The Museum of Modern Art, New York.

materials associated with painting and sculpture are visible. Finished paintings hang from the wall and are propped up around the room, and an empty frame awaits a painting. Two sculptured figures stand on their pedestals, and nearby are some paint brushes and paint pots. An easel and two empty chairs wait for artist and model, and we see a wine glass, a vase, and other items for a future still life.

Matisse's scene is familiar enough, but the artist is absent and nothing is happening. Like archaeologists we have happened upon a place where remnants of human activity are in evidence, yet we must interpret the significance of these artifacts. How well are we prepared to interpret the activity of the studio? Is our image of what occurs in studios sufficient when we define it only in *contrast* to the search for truth in the laboratory?

We may begin our interpretation of Matisse's painting confidently, believing that creative work will resume when the artist returns, for we think of the studio as a place governed by the artist's intentions and the activities that flow from them. We usually frame our account of the causality of art in subjectivist terms, treating the creative imagination of the artist as the primary source for his works. When we define the creative process in this way, the studio becomes the place where subjective intentions are transformed, almost by magic, into material form. All that counts is how skillfully the intentions become manifest. Cleverness and wit seem to be at a premium, in contrast to the disciplined intelligence of the scientist. Given these assumptions, the studio is a place where the creative mind gains its outlet and where the expressive powers of man are enhanced. On the whole, this is precisely how modern artists have viewed their own work. Nevertheless, this account of the goal of the studio is too limited. One reason why it has been accepted, by artists and nonartists alike, is the exclusive authority we give to science in matters of truth. When we do so, what is left for the studio except emotive and subjective concerns?

The purpose of the present study is to challenge the elements in our interpretive framework that limit the artist to noncognitive concerns. I will argue that artists are just as involved with truth as scientists. Although many twentieth century artists have endorsed the idea of inherent conflict between creativity and truth, we will not follow them in this judgment, which stems from questionable assuptions in an inherited philosophy of mind. These assumptions make it appear that a necessary conflict exists between creative imagination and reason. Advances in the philosophy of mind, particularly due to Wittgenstein, have made clear the need to reassess our grasp of the vocabulary of feeling and imagination. We no longer have reason to limit the artist to giving vent to his feelings or free play to his imagination. He is also an active contributor to our knowledge and understanding. In order to demonstrate this, we must raise doubts about the starting point of modern thought: the subject-object distinction. This dichotomy makes it appear that when modern artists renounce the representation of objects they must instead embrace some version of subjectivism. Insofar as modern artists have deleted references to the objective world from their work, how else shall we regard them but as the champions of subjectivity?

The only plausible alternative has been to treat art as an autonomous domain, in which the artist contributes to a specialized cultural area with little regard for anything else. His only concern is with what art's own development requires. This is the characteristic attitude of formalism, which treats modern art as a triumph of maturity because modern art explicitly features the formal concerns that have always been germane to art, even in its traditional styles. If we return to Matisse's *The Red Studio* with this view in mind, we find that our orginal description was problematic. If we read the two-dimensional surface *as* a two-dimensional surface, suppressing our habit of projecting into illusionistic depth, we can begin to view the painting in terms of purely formal relationships. Shape and color are the elements of Matisse's art, and the uniform red ground invests the "objects" of the studio with fluidity and visual dynamism. What we superficially read as familiar objects now appear to have an ambigous relationship to their visual ground. In his characteristic way Matisse displays figure-ground alternatives to us, exploiting positive and negative shapes to elicit different interpretive possibilities. His masterful economy of means confronts us with the complexity of all visual interpretations. We must add now that the studio is a place where our visual capacites may be *expanded*. Modern artists have surely enriched our visual experience precisely by the free development of formal elements that enter into their art.

While interpreters of modern art have characteristically vacillated between subjectivism and formalism, there is another alternative. As long as we fail to question assumptions which divide the world between objective reality and experience, or objective reality and culture, subjectivism and formalism will be the only alternatives that we can envision. Nevertheless, modern artists like Matisse challenge us to reconceive how the world presents itself to us and how we interpret it. Matisse's sophistication goes beyong his virtuoso mastery of visual forms, a mastery quite evident in his work and in that of other modern artists. He shows us the artist engaged in an essential human activity: picturing the world. In the following chapters we will explore some of the ramifications of how modern art challenges the scientific world view and points toward a new way of thinking. Within this context we will make generous use of the ideas of Nietzsche, Heidegger, Wittgenstein, and Merleau-Ponty, but we will use works of art as the primary sources of our analysis.

This study might well be entitled "Philosophical Investigations into Art and Culture." Where should we begin such an investigation? My answer is with the art works themselves. *The Red Studio* can act as a question-generating source. So many books in aesthetics work in the opposite direction, giving such priority to epistemology that works of art are lost in the analysis. In contrast, the present study will use specific art works as sources and continuing reference points for the investigation. *The Red Studio* speaks to us about artists and the places where they work, but it also displays features of the larger human context as well. We need to treat it as a reference point for developing a better understanding of human intentions and of the creative process.

Matisse's painting catches us on the divide between modern art and the more traditional art which precedes it, because he presents us simultaneously with objects in a room and with an active field of forces which undermine our confidence in objective understanding. In so doing, he confronts us with a central issue of twentieth century thought: the problem of the relativity of interpretations. While the relativism theme may appear to support either subjectivism or formalism when we interpret culture, another alternative exists. We usually conceive cultural forms as relativistic in either of two ways: either an individual creates unique expressive forms, which externalize his personal perceptions and feelings; or he contributes to the ongoing development of cultural history, conceived as the conventional expression of groups of people (artists of nineteenth century France, writers of eighteenth century England, European physicists of the eighteenth century, etc.). The formalist approach is often treated as one species of conventionalism (unless it is linked, as it was by some early modern artists, to transcendent knowledge).

The present study goes beyond this either/or of subjectivism and conventionalism. While accepting the relativity of interpretations as the starting point for our thinking, we will argue that relativity is no reason for despair where our interest in truth is concerned. Although historical forms give us a limited grasp of reality, they give us access to it, rather than blocking it from our view. Matisse displays the studio as a place where such limitations prevail by showing us the artist confronting his work in the context of the available materials, his own past works, and his desire to go on creating. In addition, since we know that he can create nothing without forms of expression already at hand, there is no neutral ground on which he can begin. Nevertheless, artists do succeed in picturing the world. No barrier intervenes between artist and world, except the normal limitations encountered in learning to formulate one's perceptions. Artists' works are as historical as anything can be, and that is just what enables us to comprehend them, since we share cultural meanings with them.

In this book we will resist assumptions which suggest a "veil of ideas" intervening between artist and world, or merely private feelings that create a barrier between the artist and those who view his works. Instead we begin with the artist in the studio, working within the limits of its walls, his own past works, and established cultural forms, yet striving to understand aspects of the world made accessible through these means. Great artists, as much as great philosophers and scientists, have achieved real understanding and have revealed it to others. Therefore, the prevailing schism between the laboratory and the studio cannot be allowed to remain. To argue that it needs to be reconsidered does not detract in any way from the very real achievements of science. All that it does is to reestablish a central place for the arts in our lives.

This study falls roughly into four sections. Chapter I, which raises the central question of the book, examines the connection between art and truth and poses the problem of relativism. Chapters II and III critically examine some prevailing ideas about expression and feeling, explore analogies between art and language, and expose common assumptions about the creative mind. Chapter IV, V and VI, forming the third section, present a theory of culture based on the art-language analogy and explain how this approach alters our understanding of the creative process. They also discuss how this approach changes our concept of the nature-culture relationship. Finally, Chapters VII and VIII sketch an historical account of truth, reconsider the relativism question, define a central role for imagination in our cognitive life, and consider the implications of these ideas for ethics.

The philosophical inspiration for this study is Heidegger's provocative essay, "The Origin of the Work of Art." However, the real inspiration for it is a number of great paintings—paintings particularly by Matisse, Cezanne, Rembrandt, Munch, and Hans Hofmann—which convinced me that our standard interpretations of modern art are simply inadequate. These paintings form the real starting point for these investigations, and they remain the testing ground on which it should be judged.

Thinking about these things: it is hard for me to see any differences between the scientist and the artist. They are both in search of the truth, and they must find creative ways of finding that truth and expressing it. In a sense, when the scientist finds and names something that was unknown to us before—he is creating it, just the same as the artist is searching for something he knows is already out there, but he also must find it and name it.

CHAPTER ONE

Representation and Truth

In a famous essay Heidegger chal-
lenges prevalent ideas about art when he says: "Art . . . is the becoming
and happening of truth."[1] This saying, although rich with meaning,
requires careful thought, since it is contrary to many twentieth century
assumptions. We tend to begin our thinking with the contrast between
science and other enterprises: thus, science and art. Truth is the business
of science, but not, we think, of art. Heidegger asks us to reconsider this
stance and to envision a larger role for the arts.

In a scientific age we are prone to think of truth as objective and
factual. Factual truths get formulated into propositions, which make
specific claims about the world. The sciences divide up the world for
study, refining their factual claims with the aid of specialized methods.
Methods are the key to success in these disciplines. They appear to yield
correct representations of reality, which correspond closely to the things
being studied. This correspondence theory of truth, which is deeply
etched in our thinking, contributes to a restricted understanding of the
place of the arts. The arts give us no methods for studying the world, and
so we think we must relegate them to expressing feelings. This tendency
is reinforced by modern art's renunciation of accurate representation, or

HEIDEGGER: ART IS THE
BECOMING AND HAPPENING OF
TRUTH
(A DIALECTICAL PROCESS)

naturalism, as the proper goal for the artist. We may view this shift as creating a new, subjective basis for art, leaving the field of objective study exclusively to the scientist. Because we habitually identify truth with the objective approach, the modern artist's preoccupation with expression, and seeming hostility to representational references, has sealed the fate of the arts: they are simply irrelevant to truth. Heidegger however, does not agree with this assessment. His claim calls for reflection.

Heidegger has good reason to reconsider the separation of art from truth. When we begin to question the subject-object distinction, on which this separation is based, we find it permeated with confusion. For example, applied to painting it appears to establish a watershed between the premodern and the modern, since the premodern artist made direct references to people and things, while the modern artist has frequently tried to avoid them. Therefore, we may be tempted to attribute an objective mentality to the premodern artist, viewing his pictures as attempts to create images corresponding to the things or people being depicted. This idea of correspondence between pictures and things is, however, misleading. The quick identification of representational art with an objective approach leads naturally to its opposite: the identification of expressive painting with a subjective approach. While some advocates of modern art may find this new identification attractive because it establishes a clear domain over which the artist may rule without interference from the scientist, it has the unseemly implication of separating art into two histories. The first history (premodern) takes its cue from the scientific world view, while the second (modern) is built on the discovery of art's true mission: the expression of the artist's perceptions and feelings. The plausibility of this idea appears to create a division within art, which forces the artist to choose between the divergent goals of representation and expression.

Such an account does not do justice to what we find in the art of the past. For example, let us consider a painting of Rembrandt and Lievens, called *Portrait of an Old Man* (Figure 2), now housed in the Fogg Museum. This old man has a capacity to touch us deeply, moving us to feelings of pathos and uncertainty. In his eyes we find the reflection of loneliness and vulnerability characteristic of old age. We recognize emotions that we and our loved ones share. We can identify with the human condition he represents, and we are moved by it. How shall we characterize this painting? If we begin from the distinction between representation and expression, we hardly know what to say. Rembrandt is simultaneously

Fig. 2 Rembrandt Van Rijn and Jan Lievens, *Portrait of an Old Man* (1632) Oil on oak panel, 66.9 × 50.7 cm. Bequest—Nettie G. Naumburg, Courtesy of The Fogg Art Museum, Harvard University.

What does art disclose? rather than, is it truth?

representing something to us *and* expressing deeply-held feelings about old age. We find no opposition between these two goals. That should make us pause to reflect further.

Heidegger emphasizes the need to focus on the works themselves and to think of the meanings active on the presented surface. In following his advice, we discover that Rembrandt's painting does not fit neatly into the dichotomy between objectivity and subjectivity. The portrait, which is representational, does not depend for its effect on any objective likeness between painted image and the physical model. Since we do not have the model available for comparison, this can hardly be a reasonable way to think of Rembrandt's work. The idea of Alberti's window, on which Rennaissance spatial conventions are based, turns out to be misleading in this case. Nor is our only alternative to imagine Rembrandt in front of the canvas, projecting subjective states into pictorial form. Neither description is adequate to indicate the depth of this portrait. How are we to understand its power? How does Rembrandt capture the old man's humanity and reveal his character and circumstances to us? His wordless message presents us with an understanding of old age, loneliness, vulnerability, and loss. We receive this message directly, without apparent mediation by thought. Both the mood and the features of the old man's face seem to be there on the surface. The directness of pictorial surfaces is one source for our belief that we must treat pictures either as windows onto the world or as windows opening into the artist's mind. Yet this painted surface betrays the hand of Rembrandt, whose exquisite control of his palette (shades of umber) and his brushstrokes contribute to the somber mood and to the physical appearance.

We need to consider other alternatives if we are to improve our understanding of this work. While Rembrandt's painting makes no propositional claims, the concern for truth may nevertheless be present in his work. This is what Heidegger helps us to see. He requires us to modify our belief in the correspondence theory of truth, and the consequent idea that representation concerns objective likeness. What alternative might we entertain? Heidegger asks us to consider what the work of art *discloses*.[2] Heidegger's suggestion requires that we shift from thinking of truth as correspondence to thinking of it as disclosure. Thus, the proper question to ask of Rembrandt's painting is: what does *Portrait of an Old Man* reveal?

This painting reveals an emotional context, while simultaneously
linking it to its physical setting. We find ouselves moved by the portrait,
and we also gain understanding from it. Although the old man seems to
be uniquely himself, we also see general traits of humanity in his face.
Therefore, we encounter more than a portrait of a single human being;
we encounter something universal. Rembrandt has brought alive a
portion of the world, and has opened it up for us to inspect. The face of
the old man becomes a mirror to our own humanity. Thus, when
Heidegger says: "Art . . . is the becoming and happening of truth," he
may be pointing to the way in which art can give us self-understanding.
We must now explore this idea.

Our first temptation is to think that this makes Rembrandt's
painting psychological, and so, in one sense, it is. But we must be careful
with this notion of the psychological, since our way of conceiving it is
likely to be scientific. Modern psychology aspires to be one of the factual
disciplines, giving man an understanding of himself through scientific
research. This program of research directs the study of man in a special
way, seeking to translate particular aspects of human existence into
quantified data. If we are to regard Rembrandt's painting as revealing
something about ourselves, it cannot be in this scientific way. The
painting is not in competition with modern psychology, since it presents
no quantified data to be assessed. Nor does Rembrandt give us methods
to determine our judgment. He simply presents us with an image of an
old man. The painting has the same kind of directness that characterizes
our own image when seen in the mirror. It presents us with self-
knowledge in a way that is different from the way of research.

How are we to understand the self-knowledge this painting conveys?
Perhaps we should consider parallels to philosophical reflection. On first
consideration this seems an unpromising line to follow, since modern
philosophy is preocupied with epistemological analysis. That seems far
removed from Rembrandt's concerns. However, if we turn to the ancient
tradition of Socratic questioning, we may discover an affinity between
Rembrandt's work and the work of the philosopher. We will fail to see
this affinity if we attend to the surface image alone and ask questions
about what kinds of correspondence it may have. However, if we take
Socratic questioning as our model, we derive a different result. Socratic
reasoning begins from the statment of an opinion, which it then subjects
to logical criticism. This reasoning moves between the poles created by
the orginial opinion and the limits exposed by criticism, generating a

Great works of art produce an overdetermination of
meaning — *pin down time* (?)

REPRESENTATION AND TRUTH   13

revised understanding of the topic under discussion. Such a self-reflective process may seem far removed from that of the artist. It is governed by serious questioning and criticism, and we see no immediate evidence of that kind of process when we look at a painting. The approaches of artist and philosopher seem far removed from each other, given these considerations.

And yet, are they? For one thing the results of Socratic dialectic may be as multi-faceted and as often open to various interpretations as are the images of the painter. The dialectical approach of Plato or Nietzsche, while geared toward clarification, ends up generating additional questions, which require us to go on thinking about the topic at issue. In similar fashion, a painting, although direct in impact, has a similar capacity to suggest multiple meanings and provoke further thinking. Great works of art exhibit an overdetermination of meaning; they tend to create multiple associations, which raise puzzling questions for a thoughtful viewer. Perhaps we have some reason to ponder Heidegger's understanding of art as disclosure, given this similarity in outcome between philosphical dialectics and the work of art. How can we explore this line of thinking further?

The ancient philosophical approach operates on a different basis than modern thought, which begins from the contrast between subject and object. Questions of correspondence are not central to Socratic thinking, but instead it examines a topic from the context of already formulated opinions. The topic is not treated at a distance, as part of objective reality. Justice, for example, is a topic taken from everyday life. Everyone understands something of what justice entails, even if the theory of justice is relatively obscure. If we were to view the ancient questioning activity in contemporary terms, we might describe it as an examination of the language of justice, starting from the meaning contained in our utterances about justice. In questioning the meaning of our utterances, we may gain self-awareness in our speaking by hearing what we say in a new way. Philosophy, in making us reflective about our opinions, may cause us to avoid unthoughtful utterances. By making what we say stand in relief against clearly formulated alternatives, Socratic reflection makes our presuppositions evident. Premature opinions are challenged, resulting in an enhanced awareness of the complexity of the world.

We have said that the work of art may seem antithetical to this reflective stance. Whereas the philosopher's discourse is indirect,

SOCRATIC
INQUIRY
REEXAMINE
IN LIGHT
OF
REALITY

MAKES OUR
PRESUPPOSITION
EVIDENT

art v.
philosophy

mediated as it is by reflective questioning, the artist's work seems immediate and direct. Whereas the philosopher's views must be formulated with precision, so that ambiguity is minimized, the artist seems unconcerned with precise distinctions and expresses himself in nonverbal ways. Even when the art form involves language, as in poetry, the artist's concern is with the effective image, rather than with a self-critical argument.

We will postpone until the next chapter a detailed analysis of the expressive aspect of works of art, but the contrast between art and dialectical reasoning we are noting here depends on a division between cognition and feeling that will ultimately prove deceptive. In spite of appearances to the contrary, some dialectical elements do enter into works of art. The burden of the remaining chapters will be to establish this.

For the present, we need to construct a plausible parallel between the artist's work and the philosopher's quest for self-understanding. In other words we need to reconcile the immediacy of the artistic image with the dialectical questioning of the Socratic thinker. This is the key to Heidegger's claim that art is "the becoming and happening of truth." We can only approach an answer to this question if we turn to a complete philosophical work, such as Plato's *Republic*, rather than to particular arguments it contains. The *Republic* moves from the opinions of two characters (Cephalus and Thrasymachus) about the nature of justice, and subjects these opinions to dialectical questioning. However, Plato fails to present us with a specific theory of justice in his dialogue, but gives only a series of exchanges which gravitate in a direction. Thus, the movement of the dialogue as a whole is toward refinement of our understanding of justice, through the questioning process, rather than toward a doctrine about justice. The dialectical *process*, understood in this way, is more central to the "becoming and happening of truth" about justice than any formulation of a *theory* of justice. In reading Plato's dialogues one develops the feeling that the questions posed are, in one sense, inexhaustible, insofar as each question generates a whole new chain of questions that continue to engage our attention. Therefore, we might regard the dialectical process in the *Republic* as the development of a complex image about justice.

The texture of the exchange is, therefore, essential to the form of self-understanding derived. In this philosophical approach to justice there is a curious blending of the discussion of the subject matter with a self-conscious mirroring of the process by which the discussion is carried out. We do not have a very clear parallel in the arts to this philosophical approach until the advent of modern art, but the modernist manifests the same self-consciousness as the philosopher about the way the medium is affecting the process of creation.[3]

If we think of a work like Plato's *Republic* as a whole, we find clear parallels to the images presented by the artist. Such images are always more complex than an immediate, surface reading might indicate. Thus, Rembrandt provides the viewer with a condensed image of old age, presented through the face and figure of an old man. The directness of the image nevertheless hides from our view the complicated levels of perception it embodies. This is similar to the way we obtain a single glimpse of Plato's *Republic* after reading the whole work, even though the reading of the work is a complex, time-factored process.[4] If we were to forget the process of reading his book, in the same way as we overlook the levels of perception in a visual image, then the parallel would be complete.

If the artistic image condenses complex meanings into a single symbolic form, we have discovered an important principle for our inquiry. Let us consider this principle further. We call the product of the artist's endeavor the art *work*. What kind of work is hidden by the immediately presented surface image? In part it is a thought process that has a striking parallel to the dialectical approach of the philosopher. Although the artistic process does not usually employ verbal means, it may nevertheless reflect stages of dialectical development. For example, we have a record of Picasso's painful struggles as he groped toward the final version of *Guernica*. Picasso captures the disaster in that Spanish village in a powerful condensed image, but only after he had refined his vision in many preliminary drawings. Each figure underwent significant changes before appearing in its final form in the painting. And while the final work does not directly reveal it, the preliminary drawings, watercolor drafts, and other forms of preparation, contributed in important ways to the image presented in the final version. Thus, a kind of pictorial dialectic stands behind *Guernica*.[5] And it is not, of course, idiosyncratic to Picasso to work in this way. The artist does not simply paint a portrait, a scene, or a direct set of relationships, because the nature of the work as   condensed image reflects a richer content than a surface reading of the painting would indicate. We have far more in Rembrandt's portrait than the likeness of one man. To see the portrait

why a painting is not a
snapshot

simply as a likeness is to assume that a snapshot would reveal the same thing as the painting. However, part of the expressive power of Rembrandt's portrait is that its content transcends the idea of one individual's face at a given moment of time. Picasso's *Guernica* also encapsulates something universal, even though it is launched from a particular set of circumstances in history. We shall have occasion to return to this point in Chapter VI, but the role of the universal in the condensed image is part of what seems to be indicated when Heidegger says that "art . . . is the becoming and happening of truth." We begin to see the limited understanding we have of artistic representation when we treat it as correspondence of image with thing.

We are tempted to treat the presentational surface of paintings and other works as if they exhibit simple perceptual qualities. However, the line of argument we have been following shows the inadequacy of such a concept. If a particular situation or individual is the reference point used by the artist, this concrete grounding does not become a fixed limit for the work. The principle of condensation of content into image is part of what sets a work of art apart from a craft object or a merely decorative piece. Imaginative expansion is part of what characterizes the great work. A process of dialectical development must stand behind the image we behold as a finished product. Thus, it is possible to argue that the artist's concern with the subject of his painting parallels the philosopher's quest for self-understanding.

Our understanding of the artist's intentions is changed in important respects if we accept Heidegger's idea that truth is a concern of the artist. Instead of thinking of the work as expressing a limited, subjective state, we see it now as the product of a lengthy working process, which includes both the development of thoughts and their material manifestation in the artist's medium. Acts of creativity take shape within the medium employed, and the limits of one's knowledge of color, spatial relationships, light, and paint enter as real factors that determine the outcome. The only reasonable interpretation of art works is that they result from a rough idea that is transformed and refined as the artist interacts with his materials. It is a misconception of the creative act to think of it as arising from a clear-cut intention of the artist, as if the materials employed were mere means of expression. The dynamic interaction of the artist with the medium deserves emphasis; a more realistic picture of the creative process is that after a certain amount of work is done, the artist looks at the result, considers how to go on, and then modifies the piece as seems appropriate. Just as the Socratic dialectic reveals the limits of already verbalized opinions and calls for their refinement, so the artist's preliminary sketches reveal the necessity of transforming his images into a more adequate form of pictorial expression. Active metamorphosis, rather than imposition of an intention, is what occurs in creative work.

This is not just a physical metamorphosis which the artist imposes on his materials. Instead, it demands self-development by the artist, since the feelings to be expressed are not fully conscious before the act of creation, but are born from it. The individual artist does not function as a willful, self-conscious agent, but in some other way. The following observation by Merleau-Ponty may help us to understand this better:

> The meaning of what the artist is going to say *does not exist* anywhere—not in things, which as yet have no meaning, nor in the artist himself, in his unformulated life. It summons one away from the already constituted reason in which "cultured men" are content to shut themselves, toward a reason which contains its own origins.[6]

As Merleau-Ponty sees it, self-development is required of the artist because the meaning to be created does not yet exist. If we consider, as well, his claim that the creative act moves beyond conventional rational understanding, we may be led to think of it as irrational. However, Merleau-Ponty holds that the artist formulates his meaning from "a reason which contains its own origins." How are we to understand this idea, and how does it relate to the question of representation and truth?

If we return for a moment to Matisse's *The Red Studio*, and the questions it raised for us about the artist's intentionality, we begin to find an answer. Although we were first struck by the absent artist, whose presence seemed necessary before any work could be done, we also identified other important elements in the painting. If we were to attend only to the absent artist, then we might think of creativity as a momentary act. The more we confine it to the moment the more miraculous it seems, and the more we require only the missing genius who will create something from within himself. However, Matisse also shows us a background which includes finished paintings and sculptural figures. What is their significance for our reflections? They are an already formulated context of meaning for the artist, and are available to him as sources for his new work. In other words, the artist's self-development grows naturally from his own past, and he must struggle to fit his new work into a developing, coherent vision. Thus, we can construe "a reason which contains its own origins" as reflecting this developing vision. The artist works from a set of long-term problems and develops patterns of meaning in response to them. These attempts to make sense of the world through the created pictures reflect a *cultured* vision.

This gives us additional understanding of what Heidegger may mean by "art . . . is the becoming and happening of truth." We should not regard individual works as discrete creations reflecting occasional bursts of inspiration. When we look at the life work of an artist like Matisse, we find a sustained exploration of visual questions which grow in subtlety and increase his capacity to disclose complex relationships. In the case of Matisse we observe the consistent development of an imaginative vision which challenges us to enlarge our understanding of the world and of ourselves. Thus, instead of treating pictures as correspondences to reality, we may think of them as opening up new understanding.

Although we often conceive of artistic imagination as an irrational force, we interpret it according to Merleau-Ponty's model as "a reason which contains its own origins." When viewed in this manner, a distinctive feature of imaginative vision is that it develops in its own terms rather than in terms of conventional rationality. This theme links imagination to the problem of interpretation. We need not view imagination as a force in opposition to reason, but as a particular kind of interpretative stance: one which challenges prevalent ways of viewing reality. This idea is further supported by another observation of Merleau-Ponty, concerning the cave paintings at Lascaux: *the creation of a wall*

> The animals painted on the walls of Lascaux are not there in the same way as the fissures and limestone formations. But they are not *elsewhere*. Pushed forward here, held back there, held up by the wall's mass they use so adroitly, they spread around the wall without ever breaking from their elusive moorings in it. I would be at great pains to say *where* is the painting I am looking at. For I do not look at it as I do at a thing; I do not fix it in its place. My gaze wanders in it as in the halos of Being. It is more accurate to say that I see according to it, or with it, than that I *see it*.[7]

The relationship, then, between the pictorial space and the physical space of the cave surface is not, in this view, simple or straightforward. The paintings do not use the space in the same way ordinary objects do. The essential point here is that pictorial forms help us to see something in a new way; we see *according* to them instead of seeing them in objective terms. Paintings, and other art works, provide us with frameworks for seeing and thinking which may challenge prevalent interpretations of the world. Part of the public's shock on first encountering modern art reflected the divergence of its vantage points from common interpretations of nature, human perception, and social reality. Like new metaphysical systems, works of art may provoke a revision of conceptual frameworks and awaken new sensibilities. When we encounter the cave paintings, Egyptian art, or other unfamiliar visual traditions, they may expose the limits of our own assumptions. They confront us with the variety of representations that form the natural history of mankind. Thus, we begin to understand how limited our ideas of rationality may be, and we begin to form the hypothesis that rationality is a capacity for coherent representation, in whatever form. This line of reflection suggests a more dynamic concept of truth.

The development of a variety of visual perspectives has been a hallmark of twentieth century art. Cubism, futurism, surrealism, and abstract expressionism are only some of the styles of visualization that we encounter in twentieth century painting. We have often interpreted this variety of styles as symptomatic of the artist's detachment from reality, and as an attitude which values sheer variety and novelty. However, another premise might be that twentieth century artists, like twentieth century philosophers, have gradually been developing an altered understanding of human perception and interpretation.

What this requires is a new understanding of the relationship between human agents and the world. *The Red Studio* shows us the context of the artist's *actions*; it is a context where the materials are in readiness and where he is surrounded by his own past achievements. The context is historical, and that is the actual starting point for his experiences when he returns to the studio, rather than some subjective datum of his own mind. Nothing is given as an absolute starting point for his work; there is only the studio and the challenges it presents. Matisse has shown us the actual context of creation: we can recur to habitual interpretations, which make sense of the surroundings of the studio in terms of familiar objects objectivity and subjectivity in Matisse

and familiar limits (e.g., the walls of the room); or we can loosen the hold of these familiar ways of seeing, and treat the figures as free-floating forms, whose *relationships* to each other create the context of experience. When we stop to reflect on the situation presented by Matisse, we see that not even the walls provide an absolute starting point, since there is the window, opening to the outside. Even if we choose to *take* the walls as our point of orientation, and begin from the objects they help to define, we cannot miss the relativity of our experiences to this interpretive stance. And Matisse has displayed for us precisely where the modern artist works: within a self-conscious knowledge of the relativity of any and all perspectives.

This only appears to place the artist in a subjective stance if we believe there is some privileged objective stance with which it contrasts. However, once we have seen that objectivity concerns methods of approach and standards of testing, the artist's position is no different from the scientist's. Both interpret the world from perspectives that are within the space they seek to understand. We have seen that even the distinction between interior and exterior depends on relationships that hold *between* them, rather than priority being given automatically to one over the other. What we lack is any foundational experience to provide a neutral basis for comparison.

The action context of the studio helps to make clear to us this relativity of perspectives. Each of our schemes of interpretation is a simplification. Nietzsche was, perhaps, the first philosopher to comprehend the full significance of this point.[8] For example, he argues:

> That the value of the world lies in our interpretation (—that other interpretations than merely human ones are perhaps somewhere possible—); that previous interpretations have been *perspective valuations* by virtue of which we can survive in life . . . that every elevation of man brings with it the overcoming of narrower interpretations; that every strengthening and increase of power opens up new perspectives and means believing in new horizons— this idea permeates my writings.[9]

If we take Nietzsche's idea of *perspectivism* seriously, we begin to see a new role for artistic imagination, one which concerns truth more than we at first supposed. For example, Picasso's *Woman Ironing* (Figure 3) may expose more about the burdens of women and the lower classes than a

Fig. 3   Pablo Picasso, *Woman Ironing* (1904)
Oil on canvas, 45-¾″×28-¾″. The Justin K. Thannhauser Collection, Courtesy of
The Solomon R. Guggenheim Museum, New York. Photo: Robert E. Mates.

hundred treatises on economic and social organization. The way we regard people's daily activities in our society may be modified once we feel the harshness of life symbolized by Picasso's figure: the harsh lines and angles of the woman's body, the dull grey-brown atmosphere, and the projected feeling of death all speak to the subsistence level of her daily life. Or a film like Kubrick's *2001* may clearly display parallels between our experience and that of primitive man, even though we are tempted by our technological achievements to obscure the similarities. These examples reinforce the idea that disclosure is a central purpose of the arts and that artists contribute to our understanding, in part, by exposing our perspectives as oversimplifications. Thus, imagination is not self-indulgent fancy to be classified with children's play.[10] Instead, imagination opens aspects of reality to our view, aspects we would otherwise overlook.

Nietzsche's position that our interpretations are simplifications underscores our tendency to get lost in our own abstractions, and to mistake them for concrete descriptions of reality. Alfred North Whitehead has called this the Fallacy of Misplaced Concreteness.[11] Although Whitehead coined this term to describe a tendency endemic to modern science, he warns us that it may invade all human interpretive activities. This is because we are prone to limit our understanding of the real to the set of categories with which we are most familiar, thereby failing even to notice other actual features of the world. A central role for the arts, seen in this way, is to give us concrete grounding by bringing us back to these actual features in a forceful way. We learn from the pictures we have encountered, and they remind us of the richness of the world. Once we have experienced a Cezanne landscape, for example, we begin to see our own surroundings with his eyes. Even the most abstract art, which makes no direct reference to objects or situations, helps us to see more concretely; it highlights features of the world we tend to overlook by isolating our attention on such factors as color relationships, the interaction of form with color, and the creation of negative shapes by positive shapes. After intense involvement with art works we return to the world with new eyes. We begin to see movement where there was only stasis, new nuances of color appear, and new rhythms emerge in our surroundings. Thus, the idea that picturing the world is linked only to accuracy of representation is shallow. And a subjectivist account of art, which is a reaction against the limitations associated with accuracy of representation, is equally shallow. Art is not limited to giving vent to the artist's feelings.

For this reason we have emphasized Heidegger's association of creativity with truth. However, there is one obvious difficulty about the truth theme that we must address. Our reasoning has led to prespectivism, as one consequence of the variety of visual frameworks. Is perspectivism consistent with the idea of truth? There appears to be a conflict here. If art teaches us anything about reality, doesn't it show that there are many realities? Multiple frameworks? *Ways* of seeing, rather than one way? How, then, can Heidegger speak of "the becoming and happening of truth"? Nietzsche's own perspectivism led him, on occasion, to deny that there is any truth. For example, he concluded the passage quoted above by saying:

> The world with which we are concerned is false, i.e., is not a fact but a fable and approximation on the basis of a meager sum of observations; it is "in flux," as something in a state of becoming, as a falsehood always changing but never getting near the truth: for— there is no "truth."[12]

If, with Nietzsche, we recognize the relativity of perspective, how can we escape his conclusion that "there is no truth"? Our reflections on art have led us to a paradox.

A paradox calls for further reflection. In this case, the paradox results from the juxtaposition of two ideas from quite different contexts: an absolutist concept of truth, which assumes a single account of reality, has been merged with our own reflections about the relativity of perspectives. Our twentieth century understanding not only must confront diverse cultures but also the conviction that even the broadest scientific generalizations (such as Newtonian physics) are subject to change. One alternative we have is to find a way to relinquish the absolutist approach to truth, without the concept of truth losing all significance. The task of the remaining chapters is to establish this claim.

One requirement of our study will be to address the cultural relativity of the arts directly. We will do so in Chapters III, IV, V, and VI where we will examine the concept of cultural traditions by treating them as analogous to languages. Although there is a variety of languages and ways of speaking within any given language, we are still able to speak

The truth about art is that it creates a world, but not all worlds

about the world in a reliable fashion. Even if we are unable to speak in a totally univocal way about the world, what we say is still *about* the world. In parallel fashion, picturing the world may also be possible even though we find that pictures reflect a wide variety of perspectives and styles. For our present purposes, we should simply note that Heidegger's association of creativity with truth does not require us to embrace an absolutist approach to truth. He speaks of the *becoming* of truth, not the uncovering of an already-fixed truth.

Thus, it is only with respect to a particular conception of truth and reality that Nietzsche's hyperbole ("there is no 'truth'") applies. Nietzsche's own writing features a dialectical understanding of truth, and this has been the theme of the first chapter. The human concern for truth is not limited to the scientific idea that truth equals correspondence of propositions with facts. We have seen in this chapter that active Socratic questioning has a more tentative orientation to the world; there is no expectation that a given perspective encompasses the final truth. The artist's concern is to picture the world, even though he lacks an absolute perspective. Such an idea is reflected in Merleau-Ponty's description of Cezanne:

> He considered himself powerless because he was not omnipotent, because he was not God and wanted nevertheless to portray the world, to change it completely into a spectacle, to make *visible* how the world *touches* us.[13]

That the world does touch us, and that we need to make visible and intelligible to ourselves just how it touches us, is the heart of the problem of truth in human life. Even when we recognize the relativism of our perspectives, the problem of truth remains. In the following chapters we will argue that modern art's shift away from naturalistic representation leaves its concern for truth intact.

CHAPTER TWO

Expression and Feeling

The finale of Mahler's *Tragic Symphony* plunges us immediately into conflict between romantic reverie and tragic despair. The soaring violins, which carry us on an idyllic flight, evoke feelings of joy, liberation, and serenity; but Mahler alters our mood dramatically by the intrusion of the brass and tympani, announcing the tragic theme. Fate enters to shatter our dreams. Mahler confronts us with emotional complexity by establishing a direct counterpoint between the sounds of joy and despair. His work has expressive power, and we are deeply moved. Music has an unusual capacity for direct expression of feeling. It is consonant with the movement of our emotional life. Music's power of emotional expression has become a model for the development of the modern visual arts. Modern artists have put aside the goal of naturalistic representation in favor of creative expression. How are we to understand this development?

Our spontaneous response to this change is to understand it as a shift toward subjectivity. In Chapter I we began to explore the significance of the modern artist's reversal of priorities in deemphasizing the objective world. Our immediate inclination is to interpret this development as generating an opposition between creativity and truth. Hence, if innovation and visual experimentation are dominant values in modern art, it may appear that truth has no place in the new value system. Indeed, many artists have reflected the belief that truth is irrelevant in the modern setting. The dialectical concept of truth, however, may release us from thinking that creativity and truth are opposing values. In the present chapter we will explore the idea that creative expression is the outgrowth of the artist's self-understanding. In contrast, we often think of creative expression as the willful projection of the artist's private states of feeling. This latter idea is at the core of the subjectivist understanding of modern art.

This subjectivist interpretation is linked to our starting point about the Mahler symphony. Music appears to reflect our states of feeling directly. We may attribute this to its subjective origins. Vassily Kandinsky, one of the founders of modern painting, regarded music as communicating the deepest personal concerns of the composer. In his influential book, *Concerning the Spiritual in Art*, Kandinsky calls for painters to orient their work around more authentic interests by focusing their work on "inner need" instead of material representation. Kandinsky believed that composers surpassed visual artists in expressive power because they composed their works from within themselves. Here is his argument:

> With few exceptions music has been for some centuries the art which has devoted itself not to the reproduction of natural phenomena, but rather to the expression of the artist's soul, in musical sound.
>
> A painter who finds no satisfaction in mere representation, however artistic, in his longing to express his inner life, cannot but envy the ease with which music, the most non-material of the arts today, achieves this end. He naturally seeks to apply the methods of music to his own art. And from this results that modern desire for rhythm in painting, for mathematical, abstract construction, for repeated notes of colour, for setting colour in motion.[1]

One attraction of music for Kandinsky is that is possesses an autonomy that visual creations lack, because the composer is under no obligation to represent any objective state of affairs. The composer's freedom "to express his inner life" is what Kandinsky covets for the painter. Although the alleged freedom in music may be questionable, resulting only from Kandinsky applying standards of pictorial representation to music, the important point for our purpose is that Kandinsky uses music, conceived in this way, as the model for the visual arts. In particular we note that this leads him to call for visual developments which emphasize "mathematical, abstract construction."

The freedom gained in abstract construction is reflected in Kandinsky's own work during the second decade of the century. His attempts to create a "music of painting" result in lyrical expressions of color and abstract form, which shape themselves into dynamic free-form "landscapes." For example, his *Painting with White Border*, (Figure 4) constructs a field of color relationships analogous to the complex interweaving of musical themes. The ambience of the dark red line, which begins in the upper right quadrant and crosses other lines and forms in the painting, seems almost like a musical theme that develops against the countermovement of other themes. The repetition of this same color in a line lower down in the painting, and the appearance of two spots of the same color in the lower right quadrant, are analogues to the repetition and rhythmic movement of the musical motif. Apparently, Kandinsky saw his paintings in this period as opening the door to the enrichment of our visual imagination. The parallel to music is reflected directly in such titles for his works as Composition, Fugue, and Improvisation. Kandinsky's improvisations of abstract form and color stand at the forefront of developments in modern art.

If we pause to consider Kandinsky's art theory, it is not unproblematic. In one sense, his meaning is clear enough when he urges painters to move away from "reproduction of natural phenomena" toward "the expression of the artist's soul." However, we have already seen that a painter like Rembrandt never limited himself to reproducing what he portrayed. His *Old Man* is, we have argued, *representative* of our humanity, rather than the representation, or replication, of a particular model's likeness.[2] Thus, whether an artist begins with natural phenomena seems irrelevant to the degree of expressiveness of his work. If the portrait of Rembrandt's old man has expressive depth, then the artist's soul is not an alternate source for the painting. Indeed, in Kandinsky's writing we find a basic ambiguity between two ways of understanding "inner need." On the one hand, we might interpret it as emphasizing the distinction between inner and outer, and much of what Kandinsky says about inner need would support this reading. On the other hand, he also speaks of inner need in relationship to the development of painting, and

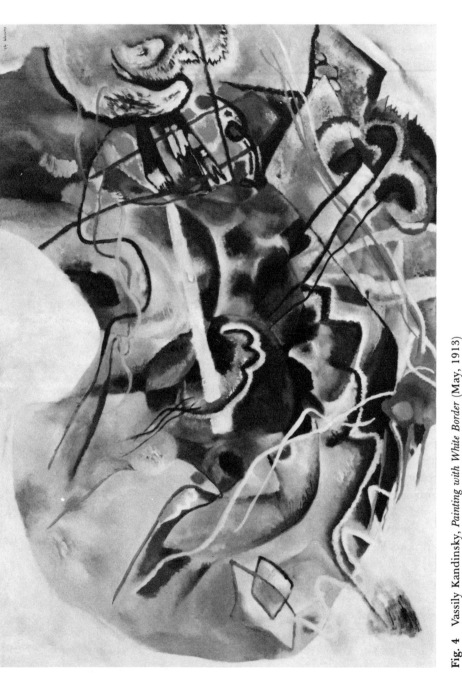

Fig. 4 Vassily Kandinsky, *Painting with White Border* (May, 1913)
Oil on canvas, 55-¼″×78-⅞″ Gift of Solomon R. Guggenheim, 1937, Courtesy of The Solomon R. Guggenheim Museum,

so he might be referring to what is required as a development internal to the subject matter of painting. We can read Kandinsky in both of these ways, but for the present we will concentrate on the first reading.

In doing so we will be viewing Kandinsky's ideas as an expression theory of the arts. The most important topic to consider is how, exactly, expression is supposed to be related to feeling. This question takes us to the heart of issues in the philosophy of mind. Kandinsky often writes as if the problem of achieving greater expressive power depends on developing expressive means that are adequate to a subjective source. Seen in this way, he is calling for two developments: a shift of attention from material reality to feelings, and an expansion of the means of expression to reflect what we encounter in our emotional life. His key assumption appears to be that we have direct access to our feelings and know what they are, if we will only attend to them. Musical composers, presumably, have attended to their feelings for a long time, and thus have developed their resources for emotional expression more fully. This subjectivist interpretation of emotions places the burden of creative expression on the enrichment of the artistic means. The ends, apparently, are already given in the artist's experiences. However, this view is seriously flawed.

Before examining the weaknesses in expressionist theories, we should note their strengths. Certainly, the emphasis on expression highlights a primary characteristic of the great work of art: its power to move us. If a work does not touch us in some direct, emotional way, we rightly question its aesthetic merit. Suzanne Langer, one of the most important of the expressionist theorists, calls this element of the work its "vital import."[3] This quality is immediately present, for example, in Matisse's *Dance* (Figure 5), which forcefully conveys a feeling of joyful abandon among the five nude dancers, circling on the grassy slope. This direct presentation of innocent joy, like Mahler's revelation of emotional conflict, is open for anyone to see and hear. We are tempted to think that the vital import of these works results from Matisse and Mahler having first experienced the emotions, after which their energy is directed to the discovery of the means of communication which, if successful, will evoke the same emotions in us. This interpretation has its appeal, and it may be that many artists have conceived of the creative process in these terms. We must modify this account in one important respect, even on first consideration, since Langer points out that what the artist expresses must

Fig. 5 Henri Matisse, *Dance* (first version) (1909, early)   Oil on canvas, 8'6-½"×12'9-½".
Gift of Nelson A. Rockefeller in honor of Alfred H. Barr Jr., Collection, The Museum of Modern Art, New York. Photo: Eric

be what he *knows* about human feeling, rather than what is actually experienced at, or immediately before, the moment of creation.[4]

This theory, which links expressive power to the achievement of vital import, arises from a particular set of assumptions about the mind of the artist and its relationship to the minds of observers. Other accounts of this relationship are possible. How can we begin to assess the adequacy of the expressionist interpretation? Let us begin by noticing the key assumption of expressionism, as contained in this passage from Langer:

> Every product of imagination—be it the intelligently organized work of an artist, or the spontaneous fabrication of a dreamer—comes to the percipient as an experience, *a qualitative direct datum*. And any emotional import conveyed by it is perceived just as directly . . . .[5]

Langer's characterization of experience in terms of "a qualitative direct datum" arises from a philosophy of mind which assumes the *givenness* of private experiential contents. In this view, the given feeling qualities are the foundation on which artistic imagination erects itself, as well as the foundation for the viewer's reception of the expressed meaning. The only difference between the givenness of an ordinary sensory experience and the givenness of a painted image is that the painted image has been projected by the artist, thereby creating an imaginary object in what Langer calls "virtual space."[6] However, the created object functions in the same direct way as the ordinary objects of physical space do in our sensory experience. We should notice that this expressionist account of art is a simple reversal of the idea of representation and the parallel correspondence theory of truth. Both treat ideas and images as the counterparts of objects in physical space. Langer's idea that the artist projects created images into "virtual space" reveals the root idea of expressionism: the artist begins with a given feeling, or knowledge of human feeling, creates the vehicle by which to express it, and (if successful) will stir the same feeling in his viewers. This makes it appear that Kandinsky's appeal for an art grounded on inner need is just a shift of the subject matter of art from outside to inside. On this interpretation *Painting with White Border* presents a psychological landscape, rather than the mundane physical landscapes of other painters. Its intensity derives from its more personal character than paintings of objects or places.

However, we should see that something has gone wrong here, and that the artist confronts a problem this theory does not even address: he must first articulate his feelings to himself, and the canvas (or other medium) serves as a surface where these feelings may emerge into self-consciousness. Feelings are not simple givens, as anyone knows who has thought at all about the process of the clarification of feelings that must be achieved by someone going through counseling.

Could it be that the expression theory rests on a crude analogy between the entities of the external world and entities which supposedly populate our mental spaces? Is this what the givenness of "a qualitative direct datum" implies? Langer's own words, quoted above, point us in another direction, toward a more critically grounded philosophy of mind, when she speaks of "the spontaneous fabrication of a dreamer" as one of the forms of imagination. In the case of the dreamer there can be no question of his choosing a means of expression for the feelings encountered in the dream. Instead the dream *is* the spontaneous unfolding of the vision, and any feelings which emerge fit into the vision without volitional control. If we were to define the dream as the *work* of the dreamer, then we might see immediate parallels to works of art. Since the dream does convey the dreamer's feelings, we have to consider that the feelings expressed by the dream are both revealed to the dreamer and created by him. This may have something to teach us about creative expression in the arts.

Of course, our temptation is to dismiss the dream case in favor of waking experience, where we often do exercise volitional control, but we should be skeptical of this move. Why? Although we usually think of the dream as a merely private vision, which has a public aspect only through groans and rapid eye movements, this retreat to privacy is not really able to address the double role of the dreamer as creator-receiver. It treats the dream as lacking a significance that it really possesses. Nietzsche has clarified the importance of dreams for our knowledge, when he observes in *The Birth of Tragedy*:

> . . . the aesthetically sensitive man stands in the same relation to the reality of dreams as the philosopher does to the reality of existence; he is a close and willing observer, for these images afford him an interpretation of life, and by reflecting on these processes he trains himself for life.[7]

Although we think of waking experience as supplying the basis for correct interpretations of life and therefore categorize dreams as part of our fantasy life, both Freud and Nietzsche have demonstrated how shallow this attitude toward dreams is. Nietzsche's account of creative imagination in *The Birth of Tragedy* insists that these visions have the power to reveal aspects of reality to us. Thus, the parallel he sees between dreams and artistic imagination is that both provide interpretations of life. The artist's activity of creating a vision may, like the dreamer's, have to unfold from within the space of the creation. This twist in our exploration undermines the idea that the creator willfully projects the image, as if he stood outside it. Langer's distinction between physical space and virtual space is not, therefore, tenable.

Our discussion of the dream image returns us to the topic of self knowledge, considered in Chapter One. Nietzsche understands the dream image, or the imaginative creations of the artist, as providing us with insights into the complexity of the psyche. This statement is easily misunderstood if we think of psychological understanding in the restricted terms of twentieth century psychology. Nietzsche's intention is to ask us to reconsider our assumptions about the mind, and to consider the possibility that we must develop a new understanding of ourselves by pondering the phenomenon of imaginative vision. Nietzsche devoted extended attention to this project in his later writings. For example, in *Twilight of the Idols*[8] he argues that we frequently confuse cause and effect when we explain human actions, particularly our own. Or rather, he points out the way in which we create a causal order for a situation we have experienced when, in fact, the situation is more complex than the causal account acknowledges. For example, the morally upright man may be stirred to indignation by the selfish behavior of another person. He takes the other person's behavior to be the cause of his indignation, which he regards as well-deserved, and over time this indignation may grow into a full-scale resentment of the selfishness of the other person. However, Nietzsche cautions us to consider that cause and effect may have been reversed in this narrative account, since it may be that deep-seated resentment is the original source of the upright man's moral commitment. Thus, while he sees the behavior of the other individual as violating his moral commitment, and therefore meriting his indignation as a consequence, Nietzsche argues that we must consider the possibility that the man's moral commitment is the result of resentments already held by him. In other words, Nietzsche asks us to consider that morality may be only the man's defense against behavior in others with which he cannot cope. Is his indignation a cause or a consequence?

This question suggests that a narrative seemingly constructed from the immediate experience of indignation may in fact reflect hidden background interests. This is precisely what the dream case suggests too, stating that our dreams have *many* interpretations beyond the one emerging in a direct narrative report. Langer's appeal to directly given qualities in art may seem innocent at first, given the fact that visual images in art are conveyed without apparent mediation. They may seem free of any narrative bias, especially since normal waking experience of a tree on the hillside, for example, provides straightforward uncontroversial descriptions. Nevertheless, the role of the visual image in a painted landscape may be more complex than it seems, and more like the moral indignation and dream experiences than like everyday visual experiences. These considerations combine to raise doubts about centering artistic expression in "a qualitative direct datum." The expression of feelings in art involves complex symbolic forms which do not necessarily show on the surface of the works.

Langer herself seems to recognize the symbolic complexity of art works, only to forget it. She takes great pains to highlight the functioning of symbol systems in human life, but she undercuts the importance of these cultural forms by tracing them back to a foundation in directly given feeling. Her approach seems to reduce symbols to the role of intermediaries between experiences; presumably the experiences are viewed as self-sufficient except for our need to communicate them from person to person. However, this gives too little credence to the deep roots even everyday experiences have in complex cultural forms. One of the ways in which symbols shape our experiences is through language. We will return to this subject later in the chapter, and in Chapter Three. For the present, however, we will consider the active way nonlinguistic symbols enter as formative factors into the life of feeling.

If we think of feelings only as momentary eruptions within experience, we will miss the dynamic contribution of the symbolic background to the formation of our feelings. For example, when I hear the Sea Interludes from Benjamin Britten's *Peter Grimes*, the intensity of the music may provoke specific feelings of fear and excitement, like those experienced by sailors in danger in a storm. The power of the music to convey these emotions is evident. However, we are prone to forget that complex associations help to shape the listener's response to the music. The listener has past experience with music, knowing that certain sounds can be made similar to the sounds of the sea, and Britten exploits these factors in composing *Peter Grimes*. In addition, the listener's general knowledge of sailing and its danger forms a silent context for the music's effect. These all contribute to the general atmosphere within which the listener's feelings of fear and excitement erupt.

Therefore, a dimension of generality enters into the special feeling tone of a momentary experience. This is surely as true for the creator as for his audience. Another remark of Nietzsche's helps us to put this point in perspective, when he observes of Schiller: "He confessed that before the act of creation he did not have before him or within him any series of images in a causal arrangement, but rather a *musical mood*."[9] In other words, Nietzsche's observation about Schiller requires that we consider the possibility that a general framework precedes, and is active in, the formation of specific feelings. For Schiller the specific images follow after the general mood. The mood is a relatively vague direction, providing the matrix within which specific images may be developed. This process of the *becoming* of feeling, from within a context of general meaning, contrasts with the notion that works of art begin from given particular feelings.

The struggle to articulate a mood into a more specific expressive form may be illustrated further by Edvard Munch's painting, *The Sick Child* (Figure 6). We must consider the fact that for Munch this painting reflects a framework of personal tragedy that hovered over his childhood, with the early death of his mother, his sister's death in her teen years, and his own prolonged illness. This framework of meaning is the general impetus that stands behind the painting. Yet Munch was unable to render the subject directly, for he tells us that he spent about a year working on the painting.[10] This is because Nietzsche's observation about Schiller applies here as well. Although Munch was surely well acquainted with the atmosphere of tragedy that pervaded his home, this did not mean that his own comprehension of it required no self-reflection. Here is what Munch himself says about the painting:

Fig. 6 Edvard Munch, *The Sick Child* (1885-86)
Oil on canvas, 119.5×118.5 cm. Courtesy of The Nasjonalgalleriet, Oslo. Photo:
Jacques Lathion.

—As far as the sick child is concerned I might tell you that this was a time which I refer to as the "pillow period." There were many painters who painted sick children against a pillow—but it was after all not the subject that made my sick child.

No, in sick child . . . no other influence was possible than that which of itself wells forth from my home. These pictures were my childhood and my home. He who really knew the conditions in my home—would understand that there could be no other outside influence than that which might have had importance as midwifery. . . . This was during the pillow era. The sick bed era, the bed era and the comforter era, let it go at that. But I insist that there hardly was one of those painters who in such a way had lived through his subject to the last cry of pain as I did my sick child. For it wasn't just I who sat there, it was all my loved ones.[11]

Munch expresses his personal ordeal in the painting, and we, the viewers identify with its emotional thrust. We feel the pain, the loneliness, and the weight of tragedy in the image Munch created. But he had to create it for himself, as well as for us. He conveys these feelings to us through a color tone dominated by greys—there are blue-greys and green greys— and by the washed out appearance of the background. In the profile of the girl against the pillow the red of her hair contrasts with the gaunt outline of her pale face against the grey-white pillow. Life and death are symbolized together in this profile. The figure of the mother, with head bent low before her fate, reaches out to comfort the child. These forms articulate a complex symbolic meaning to us, and Munch struggled for a year to condense his understanding of the actuality of the pain into this image.

If we reflect about the significance of this painting for our inquiry, what are we to conclude? The painter's struggle to create the right image entails more than fitting an expressive means to an already finished feeling. The general mood of tragedy and despair, which haunted Munch, required clarification. The painting of *The Sick Child*, by Munch's own estimate, was crucial to his development as a painter. In part, he meant that it was crucial to his technical development, but we cannot detach the style he evolved from the need to clarify the events of his life. The profile of the young girl in the painting had to fit with his understanding in a certain way for him to bring the painting to completion.

Thus, the painting was inspired by Munch's experience of his own family, and it represents the reality of his situation and expresses the emotions which grew out of it. We must think carefully if we are not to be misled by this example. Munch did not represent the reality of his situation by painting a literal narrative of his sister's death, because the figure beside the bed, who appears to be the child's mother, could not be his own mother, since she died several years before his sister. When we say that the painting represents Munch's family, we do not mean that it replicates the scene of his sister's death as he remembered it. Instead, it conveys the *meaning* which Munch developed out of his life experiences, and out of his attempt to visualize their significance. In rendering his understanding by the painted image, he establishes his personal meaning in terms which have general significance for us all, since we can identify our fate with the vulnerable figures he portrayed. If the act of creation begins, as Nietzsche suggested, with a musical mood, its articulation requires time and imaginative development. The process of working on the painting contributes self-knowledge to the painter, which he lacked when he began.

Therefore, we conclude that expression is not a matter of the invention of ingenious means to reveal an already finished feeling. Feelings form themselves out of relatively vague backgrounds and undergo transformations as they develop. They are not entities that we can look up in our psychological ledger, nor do they exist as things in the private chamber of the mind. They are life forms which undergo change and development in conjunction with our actions. For the painter or sculptor, this means that the feelings gain in depth in the process of their expression in the medium, and the artist's decisions about how to go on developing the work emerge in response to what has already been created. In the case of Munch's painting the final relationships between mother and child, the curtain, the glass on the table, and other elements of the painting were subject to numerous changes before the original impetus for the painting was satisfied.

We now understand the inadequacy of the subjectivist account of expression, which emphasizes the willful manipulation of the medium by the artist. Even when we think of a painter like Picasso, whose frequent visual experiments come closest to confirming the model of the willful manipulator, we have reason to doubt the subjectivist inter-pretation. Hans Hess, in commenting on Picasso's work, brings out another dimension of his experiments:

Picasso's work is the mirror of the world seen and experienced by him and him alone, and though it appears that he was a very willful painter who forced his subjects into the shapes he intended, he was at the same time a very humble man who looked in silence at the world.[12]

Hess' emphasis on Picasso's receptivity, his openness to what the world had to teach him, is a theme that helps us develop a more adequate interpretation of the artist's intentions as an alternative to modern subjectivism. We begin to see the importance of thinking of the artist at work within the world, instead of on the subjective side of the subject-object divide. The attitude attributed to Picasso by Hess, by which he "looked in silence at the world," is one which highlights an intention to seek self-development, to materialize his work and himself from the life situations in which he found himself. Although most of us approach our life situations within conventional limits, the artist cultivates possibilities which change these limits. They help to create new forms of feeling, and thereby enrich the emotional texture of human life. Langer seems to recognize this when she observes, in passing, that "our emotions are largely Shakespeare's poetry."[13] She might have added that our emotions are formed by Beethoven's music, by Rembrandt's paintings, by Cezanne, and a host of other artists. Instead of works of art being characterized as "the creation of perceptible forms expressive of human feeling,"[14] Langer should have said that works of art *create* forms of feeling. If we understand creativity as requiring a cultivated openness to new forms of relationship, rather than as willful projection of an already constituted vantage point, we are closer to understanding it as we should.

Thus, the perspectivism that was central in Chapter I is not to be conceived in a purely individualist way. We have already argued that the expression of feelings in art works reflects general forms of meaning, which are communally shared. This is so since the very content of an artist's experience of a situation, as we have seen in the case of Munch, gets shaped by communal meaning. Beginning from the contents already at hand, the artist works to transform them to reflect his own perspective, which exists only in relationship to the already established meanings. This process of creating new forms of feeling within an already established context of meaning can be seen at work in Matisse's painting, *Dance*. This painting, striking in its simplicity, has an elemental purity that exposes aspects of our relationship to the world often overlooked by modern man. Matisse conveys our direct involvement with nature and other people. We understand immediately that the emotional state of joyful abandon, to which we referred earlier, is the result, in part, of the unity of the circling dancers with their cosmic setting. Like children at play, they are at one with their world. The elements composing their world are three color types and a few simple bodily forms. In speaking about this painting, Matisse said in an interview: "We work toward serenity through simplification of ideas and of form. The ensemble is our only ideal. Details lessen the purity of the lines and harm the emotional intensity; we reject them."[15] Matisse sees himself as heightening emotional intensity by reducing the means of representation to a minimum. How does his style succeed in creating this intensity?

Part of the answer lies in Matisse's calling into question prevalent visual meanings, by stripping away the visual details we have come to expect. Matisse entices us to get back to the body's essential involvement in its living space by stripping away irrelevant detail. The dancers' bodies exemplify joyful abandon by their gestures, whose force is heightened by the scale of the painting (more than 8' by 12'). This scale draws the viewer into the symbolized movement of the painted figures, and a feeling of freedom and release is the result. Would this same expressive potential be realized without the contrast between Matisse's style and more familiar styles of visualizing dancers (e.g., Degas' ballerinas)? Matisse's way of exposing our direct involvement in the world, by stripping away irrelevant details, is reminscent of the phenomenologist's efforts to bring us back to the things themselves, by bracketing out familiar interpretations. The way Matisse opens up emotional possibilities often overlooked by modern man illustrates the importance of the contrast between a presented image and a background of expected meanings.

In our observations about Matisse, we referred to an idea that will prove important for our later chapters: we said that the dancers *exemplify* joyful abandon by their bodily gestures. The importance of the concept of exemplification for interpreting art has been featured in the writings of Nelson Goodman.[16] He holds that while verbal descriptions denote the things they describe, works of art differ from verbal descriptions by exemplifying the qualities they convey. A nonartistic example will get us started on understanding his analysis. Goodman points out that a sample of cloth exemplifies, or is representative of, the bolt of cloth from which it comes. It can serve as a sample because it possesses some of the same properties as the original bolt. When someone orders from a sample, however, he does not expect that every feature of the cloth he receives will be the same as the sample. The size, for example, will be different, and the purchaser would rightly be enraged if it weren't.[17] We expect the sample to have the same color, texture, and type of material as the cloth purchased, but other properties of the sample are expected to differ. Goodman argues that works of art make symbolic interpretations of human experience or the world, by exemplifying those features rather than referring to them. Thus, Rembrandt's *Old Man* metaphorically possesses the property of sadness which we experience when we encounter the old man's face.

Viewed in this way, Matisse's dancers are elemental samples of human involvement in the world. Neither their bodies, the hill, nor the sky possess all of the properties in detail that an anatomical description or physical description would include. Yet they symbolize these realities effectively, and reveal relationships which more complete descriptions or illustrations might obscure. Mattisse's purpose is to selectively focus on a few properties, in order to convey his understanding of a certain kind of human involvement in the world. While his figures on the hillside would never serve as illustrations in a scientific textbook, their deficiency for scientific purposes may be essential to their artistic success. In parallel fashion we noted how Munch's *Sick Child* is representative of his own family's situation, without giving a literally correct representation of the bedroom of his sister. Nevertheless, the painting exemplifies features of his sister's death which help us to feel its force.

For our present purposes it is enough to have noticed the link between the expressive power of art works and the background meanings they exemplify. In other words, the skilled artist condenses meaning into his painting, and this is possible because the work produced falls within larger systems of meaning that give the new painting its symbolic force. Expressive power derives, therefore, from the place of a pictorial symbol within a larger cultural system. Even if we were to follow expressionist theorists in tracing works to a psychological source in the artist, our version would display the artist's mental states as themselves functionally dependent on that same cultural system. Moreover, this dependency is characteristic of the *content* of the psychological states and not merely of their mode of expression.

If we return to Kandinsky's call for visual artists to base their work on inner need, we see that the first interpretation considered, which favored inner feeling over outer objects as the orientation point for painting, is completely untenable. We have brought to light several confusions, all of which undermine the plausibility of this idea. Our fundamental challenge has been to question the philosophy of mind on which it is based. Although Kandinsky favored a more personal art than the art of landscapes, still lifes, and portraits, we have offered an alternative account of how art may be personal. We have seen that Munch created expressive works by exploring his personal history and confronting the meaning of that history; and we have seen how the finished works exemplify the meanings that he discovered. We have also seen that *Dance*, although representing material bodies in space, also derives its expressive power from its disclosure of elemental meanings.

This leaves the second interpretation of inner need as a subject to be examined. We considered the possibility that Kandinsky thought the autonomous development of painting could occur by painters directing their attention to new techniques and the enrichment of existing visual resources. His envy of music stemmed, in part, from the high state of its technical development. Kandinsky's own emphasis on "abstract, math-ematical construction" lends credence to this reading of his text. The emphasis on abstraction and construction has certainly been central to the development of twentieth century art. Formalism, as the leading theory for interpreting these developments, will recieve special attention in later chapters. For the present, we will think of the enrichment of visual techniques in more general terms. In the broadest terms we may think of Kandinsky as calling for the expansion of the range of artistic styles, beyond the restricted forms of classic Renaissance perspective or of Impressionism. We can see that his *Painting with White Border* is an imaginative stylistic breakthrough, although it retains relationships to earlier kinds of visualizations. For example, the interaction of lines of force sets up rhythmic movements that seem to exemplify activities in physical space, even though no objects are identifiable.

The topic of artistic style links up with our earlier discussion of the artist's self-development. We have emphasized that the artist's inter-action with the medium is central to the creative process. In the case of Munch, we also saw that subject matter and style are not separable factors. His struggle to articulate the meaning of his own past required the development of a particular style of visualization. We saw, as well, that Munch moved on from his first study of *The Sick Child* to other versions of the same subject. More importantly, he goes on to apply the style developed for that study to other subjects. Although he could not have known this in advance, the new stylistic direction proved to be fruitful for his later work. Style, viewed in this way, is integral to the artist's whole life, and can only emerge gradually from the working process and the artist's criticism of what he has done. Inner need, then, can only be defined in terms of what the subject matter requires of the artist, what the history of his own development demands, and whatever limits there may be in the medium. When the artist pushes his development forward, in response to these factors, he later "finds himself endowed with new organs."[18] This idea of Merleau-Ponty interprets style as an organic development, which links the artist's work to the history of developments in his medium and to his own personal history. Like the pianist's repertoire, the artist's expressive powers may grow and be refined by continued application and by continued exercise of critical judgment.

Kandinsky's call for a "music of painting," viewed in these terms, becomes a call for stylistic developments and for expansion of the subject matter of painting. One major result of twentieth century painting has been the enrichment of the alternatives open to the painter. We must note, however, that these developments reflect the growth of the cultural tradition of painting. They are at once technical, conceptual, and expressive developments in pictorial culture. To make sense of these developments, we need not fall back on a separation between feelings and concepts, nor a separation between subject and object.

Our reflections above have been guided by Nietzsche's perspectivism, and his understanding of how deeply our thinking and feeling are embedded in symbolic forms. Instead of thinking of the Cartesian idea of the mind as a private theater of ideas, which reflects the outside world either well or poorly, we must each think of our psyche as actively forming itself within a world of symbols. We find ourselves surrounded by culture and formulating our beliefs and emotional reactions within the framework of culture. Inevitably our culture colors our encounters with new situations. Paul Ricoeur gives emphatic expression to this idea when he speaks of a "primitive connection between the act of existing and the signs we deploy in our works; reflection must become interpretation because I cannot grasp the act of existing except in signs scattered in the world."[19] Because of this intimate involvement of the artist's style and forms of expression with his culture, we will portray the visual arts in succeeding chapters in terms of the idea of visual languages. We will emphasize the role of historical traditions and communities, instead of conceiving of creativity as the achievement of an isolated individual. We are now translating Kandinsky's call for a "music of painting" as a call for the development of a higher form of visual culture.

Our view of the way feelings enter into works of art has been greatly modified by the reasoning in this chapter. We have rejected the idea that feelings can be conceived as directly given qualities. We must consider one other difficulty that appears to be unresolved by our previous analysis: although we have emphasized the relativity of feelings to the cultural background, they, nevertheless, seem to be direct. Why is it that Mahler's symphony touches us directly, and the joyful abandon of Matisse's dancers is evident for anyone who has eyes to see? Ludwig Wittgenstein's analysis of emotions and their expression will help us to join together the theme of the directness of feeling with the culture theme. To begin with, let us consider Wittgenstein's distinction between feelings of pain, which are localized in particular bodily regions, and emotions, which are not. Here is Wittgenstein's observation:

> "I feel great joy"—Where?—that sounds like nonsense. And yet one does say "I feel a joyful agitation in my breast".—But why is joy not localized? Is it because it is distributed over the whole body? Even where the feeling that arouses joy is localized, joy is not: if for example we rejoice in the smell of a flower.—Joy is manifested in facial expressions, in behavior. (But we do not say that we are joyful in our faces.)[20]

We must remember the importance of facial expressions as expressions of emotion. Our faces are the primary natural vehicles of expression for our feelings. These expressions are not normally under conscious control. We have difficulty masking our feelings from other people, especially from our friends. Eyes and faces are windows to our emotions, and so is our behavior. Mirrors reveal much to us about our own emotional condition, and we are even, on occasion, surprised by our own behavior. If we were to think of artistic expression as an extension of these natural, spontaneous forms of expression, which flow from us as easily as gestures, we would have a promising direction for a theory of creativity. The directness of artistic images, then, would be conceived after the analogue of the directness of facial expressions and behavior. All of us are practiced at interpretation of facial expressions and behavior (nonverbal communication). We learn these expressions and forms of behavior in our cultural setting, and they become second nature to us. Because of these, we overlook the fact that they are interpretations all the same. Perhaps this explains the ease with which we can read Matisse's image of the dancers. Although the faces of only two of the dancers show, and those give us very little visual guidance, the whole bodily posture and movement of the dancers unmistakably conveys feelings of joy and freedom. The easy flow of their bodies, the lightness of their step, the spontaneous whirl of their momentum, and the position of their hands all readily contribute to this interpretation. Wittgenstein asks us to consider whether any other evidence is needed for us to understand emotions. He believes that we normally assess emotions by linking behavior and setting together.[21] We do not begin with the givenness of joy, only later to infer joy in other people from our own private encounter with it. Instead, Wittgenstein holds that we learn about joy in a public way, from faces and actions of other people, and from characteristic kinds of settings. By these means we learn to identify joy in our own experience. Our understanding of joy is not the result of instantaneous recognition of it in our private experience.

We understand the application of this point to the arts, when Wittgenstein, observes:

The content of an emotion—here one imagines something like a *picture*, or something of which a picture can be made. (The darkness of depression which descends on a man, the flames of anger.)
The human face too might be called such a picture and its alterations might represent the *course* of a passion.[22]

Wittgenstein challenges us to give up the idea that emotional contents are givens. They may seem to be because we have become expert at identifying them immediately. However, we have also become expert at the immediate identification of houses, people, and animals in our own neighborhoods, just as it is easy to identify shops and streets in a familiar city. The immediacy of these identifications obscures the functioning of the complex symbols employed in making them. This complexity becomes evident only when we try to teach a child or a visitor something that is a part of our daily practices. Consider, for example, the difficulty of teaching someone to drive a car. We may never have to think about stages of movement in shifting gears because it becomes a single motion for the accomplished driver, but the novice driver must divide it into several aspects.

If this line of reasoning is sound, we can see that the expressive character of works of art seems direct because they are linked to cultural understandings which have come to seem natural. If we follow Wittgenstein's clue, and think of faces as pictures of feelings, then we begin to get a more reliable way to understand artistic expression. At this point we must be careful not to think of pictures as photographic replicas. If we think of facial expressions and forms of behavior as *cultured* activities, which exhibit feelings more or less directly, then we see artistic creation in new terms. We come to understand artistic creation in terms of the making of surfaces which resemble surfaces we are already skilled at reading, or which purposely violate conventional meanings.

Rosalind Krauss has made a similar point in discussing the expressive force of Rodin's sculpture. In considering his rendering of *Adam* (Figure 7) for *The Gates of Hell*, Krauss observes that the posture of Rodin's *Adam* is unintelligible from the standpint of normal causality and our normal understanding of events in narrative time. Although traditional sculpture had emphasized allusions to movements in ordinary space and time, by skillful managment of the relationship between figures and their backgrounds, Rodin departs from these sculptural conventions. In doing so, his figures gain expressive force. Krauss asks:

What outward cause produces this torment of bearing in the *Adam*? What internal armature can one imagine, as one looks on from the outside, to explain the possibilities of their distention? Again one feels backed against a wall of unintelligibility. For it is not as though there is a *different* viewpoint one could seek from which to find those answers. Except one; and that is not exactly a *place* from which to look at the work—any of Rodin's work—but, rather, a condition. This condition might be called a belief in the manifest intelligibility of *surfaces*, and that entails relinquishing certain notions of cause as it relates to meaning, or accepting the possibility of meaning without the proof or verification of cause. It would mean accepting effects themselves as self-explanatory—as significant even in the absence of what one might think of as the logical background from which they emerge.[23]

Krauss's emphasis on the importance of surfaces as the location of meaning in Rodin's work fits neatly with the theory of expressive meaning we have been developing with Wittgenstein's help. What Krauss calls the "manifest intelligibility of surfaces" is the feature of our experience that has been exploited by modern artists.[24] Abstract expressionism relied on this intelligibility of surfaces for its expansion of the painter's range of expression.

The intelligibility of surfaces is dependent, of course, on conventions of pictorial form that the artist finds already established. If an artist wishes to create a certain atmosphere, this atmosphere can only be made intelligible against the background conditions of those conventions, or through the modification of them. The mastery of the medium by someone like Matisse is comparable to the masterful creation of facial masks by someone expert at mime, or someone practiced at hiding their emotions. A person may have learned, for example, to put on a mask of joy when deeply uncomfortable. He can make his face stand for joy, even as Matisse's image of the dancers does. Representing or expressing an emotion in a painting is no different, in principle, for the practiced painter than for the practiced presenter of a mask. In both cases a surface is presented skillfully to observers for a particular effect. And in both cases, successful presentation depends on skillful management and modification of conventional understandings and practices.

The power to express also depends on the nature of the medium. When Kandinsky called for a "music of painting," he may have overlooked the fact that music gains its power, in part, from its ability to surround us. A musical performance has a tendency to pervade our entire environment. The medium itself has something to do with music's expressive power, rather than its superior development as an art form. Nevertheless, we should note that developments in twentieth century painting, influenced greatly by Kandinsky's ideas, have challenged the limits of the medium of painting by moving toward larger and larger canvases that have the effect of including the viewer within the field of the painting. In parallel fashion recent developments in environmental art and performance art have resulted in the further involvement of

Fig. 7 Auguste Rodin, *Adam* (1880)
Bronze, 75-½″ × 29-½″ × 29-½″. Musee Rodin, Paris, Courtesy of Rosenthal Art
Slides.

specators in the art work. These developments of the visual culture may, indeed, result in enhanced capacities for the visual artist to be expressive. However, they also raise questions about how well their creators understand the link between expressive forms and their cultural context. In some cases, certain twentieth century emphases on "inner need" have come close to a form of narcissism.

In this chapter we have moved from a theory of expression which assumes the existence of foundational feelings, to an understanding of expression which links it to culture. We have portrayed the artist's development of expressive abilities as developments in the artist's self-understanding within the cultural context. This does not mean, of course, that when Matisse effectively presents us with the feeling of joy that a complex intellectual process intervenes between us and our grasp of the presented emotion. However, we have rejected expressionist theories because they perpetuate the dichotomies between the inner and outer world, between subject and object, and between mind and body. In rejecting the goal of creating convincing illusions of external objects, many artists have seen the alternative as a turn inward. This is reflected, for example, in the strange images created by surrealists, who often talked as if they were presenting images of entities populating our secret psychological spaces. However, if Wittgenstein's analysis is correct, this turn inward rests on a mistake. It is no wonder that the entities portrayed by surrealists strike us as coming from another world, a science-fiction world rather than from our own psyche. This is because the psychological world is the world of our everyday lives. The emotions exposed to us by Mahler, Britten, Munch, Kandinsky, and Matisse do not reflect strange internal *things*, but conditions of our existence in the everyday world, as we respond to the faces and behavior of other people. Wittgenstein summarizes this point succinctly:

> "But I do have a real *feeling* of joy!" Yes, when you are glad you really are glad. And of course joy is not joyful behavior, nor yet a feeling round the corners of the mouth and eyes.
> "But 'joy' surely designates an inward thing." No. "Joy" designates nothing at all. Neither any inward nor any outward thing.[25]

Although Wittgenstein's concluding statement may strike us as paradoxical, his central point is that we should see joy as real, though not as a thing. It does not have definite boundaries, like things have, and it may be manifested in a wide variety of ways. Nevertheless, there are typical ways in which it is manifested in our experience, and the artist's creations are relative to those ways. Since concepts like joy are open-ended, (because they lack definite boundaries), our forms of expressing them include possibilities yet to be created, which we will learn to recognize after the fact.

Concepts such as joy are open-ended becuase they arise from a context of meaning which is rich and multifaceted. If we recall Ricoeur's idea that we "cannot grasp the act of existing except in signs scattered in the world," we can see that the interpretation of emotion requires us to consider these larger questions of meaning. Faces and pictures reflect meanings which are embedded in language. Although we think of culture in terms of a division between the pictorial and the linguistic, we will argue in later chapters that such a division is untenable. The natural expressive activities of daily living include both verbal and nonverbal aspects, and they are not separated from each other by any unbridgeable gulf. In fact, we will offer an interpretation which treats culture as language-like, thereby relocating emotional expression to a position parallel with verbal expression.

If we begin to test out the idea that feelings may be associated with linguistic meanings, where does this lead? The spontaneity of emotional expression of which Wittgenstein spoke has its analogue in language. I am able to marshall linguistic resources accumulated over many years of speaking, reading, and writing with little effort. The shaping influence language has on my ways of thinking is evident. Yet language is not a thing, or a collection of thing-like strings. Somehow, English as a whole enters into my thinking and speech in ways I cannot trace, and I cannot even think of the world apart from ways of speaking about it that have become second nature to me. And so it is with my feelings and the expressive movements of gestures, faces, and tones of voice. The structure of my psyche is colored by English, and the structure of my emotions by the behavior and responses I have encountered. Merleau-Ponty summarizes the kind of view we will be developing in later chapters when he speaks of language and culture:

> Through the action of culture I take up my dwelling in lives which are not mine . . . . Just as by the thick and living presence of my body, in one fell swoop I take up my dwelling in space. And like the

functioning of the body, that of words or paintings remains obscure to me. The words, lines, and colors which express me come out of me as gestures. They are torn from me by what I want to say as my gestures are by what I want to do. In this sense, there is in all expression a spontaneity which will not tolerate any commands, not even those which I would like to give myself.[26]

The spontaneity of the creative process, of which Merleau-Ponty speaks, reflects deeper roots than subjectivist interpretations allow. It is the same kind of spontaneity I have when I speak. In the next three chapters, we will consider the advantages of thinking of visual creation in terms of the idea of visual languages.

CHAPTER THREE

Vision and Language

Matisse's *The Red Studio* provided
the starting point of our study by raising questions about the artist's
intentions. The empty studio tends to evoke the image of the creative
genius, whose presence would add the missing element for the renewal
of creative work. Our analysis has shown, however, just how misleading
this idea of the creative genius may be. If viewed in the fashion of
modern subjectivism, the feelings and will of the individual creator are
the chief sources for the works. Such a view runs the risk of detaching the
artist's activities from their cultural setting. Although we must incorporate the spontaneous contributions of the artist into our account of
creative expression, a more promising image of the artist is supplied by
Heidegger when he characterizes creation as "a drawing, as of water
from a spring."[1] Just as the water surfacing at the opening reveals the
underground sources of the spring, so must we think of the artist's work
as revealing cultural sources whose presence we may easily overlook.
Nevertheless, they are essential elements in the creative process.

If we think in terms of Heidegger's image of the spring, we move
toward a more organic conception of artistic expression, according to
which created works are the spontaneous outcome of the artist's
cultivated practices. In the present chapter we will compare the artist's

activities to linguistic practices. Just as an individual's speech acts depend upon community linguistic practices, so do the individual artist's pictures reflect background visual practices. The comparison of art to language is found in one of E. H. Gombrich's books, where he writes:

> . . . I consider it a heresy to think that any painting as such records a sense impression or a feeling. All human communication is through symbols, through the medium of language, and the more articulate that language the greater the chance for the message to get through.[2]

Like Gombrich, we oppose the idea that art works are records of the artist's feelings. Although the quoted passage emphasizes the importance of symbols for communication, we will not limit our treatment of visual languages to the question of communication in what follows.

Before pursuing the idea of visual language, we must note the apparent implausibility of this idea, since many twentieth century artists have seen art as opposed to language. Whereas language is bound by grammatical and semantical rules, the artist's expressions are supposed to reflect freedom and spontaneous response. If art lacks spontaneity, it is dead. Thus, it appears to be the opposite of a rule-guided activity. As Susan Sontag has observed, a significant number of modern artists have deliberately appealed to silence, in order to escape the abstractness of language and to overcome the historical contamination that they believe it bears within itself.[3] For these artists the intuitive development of art stands in opposition to discursive reason: discursive reason is the enemy to be overcome.

But overcome by what? The concept of intuition has many different interpretations, and we need to pause to consider what it may imply. Langer, for example, speaks of intuition in these terms:

> . . . I do believe, with many aestheticians and most artists, that artistic perception is intuitive, a matter of direct insight and not a product of discursive thinking . . . . It does not involve belief, nor lead to the acceptance of any proposition at all. But neither is it irrational, a special talent for making a mystical, unnegotiated contact with reality. I submit that it is an act of understanding, mediated by a single symbol, which is the created, visual, poetic, musical or other aesthetic impression—the apparition that results from the artist's work.[4]

This version of artistic intuition emphasizes direct insight, conveyed by a single symbol. The governing contrast is between intuition and the multiple logical steps of discursive reason. However, Langer also opposes concepts of intuition which are irrational and feature "mystical, unnegotiated contact with reality." Some of the artists referred to by Sontag regarded their appeal to silence as reflecting just such a transcendence of rationality and the material world. For example, artists like Rothko and Newman, who developed a style sometimes called the abstract sublime, thought in terms of transcendent intuitions.

Langer's emphasis on "an act of understanding, mediated by a single symbol," gives us another version. Perhaps we can clarify her idea by considering Munch's striking painting titled *Madonna* (Figure 8). In this painting Munch creates a condensed image of his understanding of women. He provides an impression of seductive alienation through a single, complex symbol. His naked figure is sensuous, mysterious, and receptive, but at the same time, dangerous, distant, and unyielding. She is both exalted and debased, resonating with the overtones of the madonna and the prostitute. Munch's painting suggests the power of women to encompass, absorb, and destroy a man's identity, yet it also symbolizes woman as the source of life and the prime example of our connection with the earth. The sweep of the madonna's hair merges with the surrounding, uncomprehended void. The whirl of the void mirrors the whirl of the strands of her hair. The sun appears as a source of light hidden by her head, but also forms a halo for her. The color of the sunset pervades the background and appears to form itself into bloodlines supplying her with nourishment. She is at one with the earth, merging with its Dionysian forces to generate her seductive spell.

How does this painting help us to grasp the concept of artistic intuition? For one thing, we can see that Munch's understanding of womanhood is not reducible to a simple set of propositional claims. Although the image is singular, it contains multiple, conflicting strands of meaning. It rewards our continued approaches, as we return to reflect on it again and again. It reveals Munch's own response to women, even as it may conflict with aspects of our own. But it reveals more than a personal vantage point, since it also exposes ingrained attitudes of our cultural condition, reflecting aspects of our responses to motherhood, sexuality, and the social subservience of women. All of this information is conveyed to us through the visual symbol, illustrating what Langer meant by an "act of understanding, mediated by a single symbol." We

Fig. 8 Edvard Munch *Madonna* (1893–94) Oil on canvas, 35½″ × 27″.
Courtesy of Munch Museet, Oslo.

gain this information from Munch's painting more or less directly, without translating it into the terms of discursive reason.

Because multiple meanings are condensed into a single image, paintings may have an absorbing intensity that leads to prolonged investigation of their surfaces. Art works present us with a problem of interpretation just because of their compressed complexity. From the standpoint of discursive reason, we may think of this complexity as a form of ambiguity. Such an idea is reflected in one of Leonard Bernstein's comments on the music of Mozart:

> . . . through this perfect combination of opposites, chromaticism and diatonicism, there is distilled the essence of ambiguity. Now this word "ambiguity" may seem the most unlikely word to use in speaking of a Golden Age composer like Mozart, a master of clarity and precision. But ambiguity has always inhabited musical art (indeed, all the arts), because it is one of art's most potent aesthetic functions. The more ambiguous, the more expressive, up to a certain point. Of course, there's a limit. . . . [5]

Although Bernstein speaks here of ambiguity, we may be better served to think of the multiple meanings of art works in other terms. Wolfgang Iser has given the right emphasis when he argues that the writer, or other artist, exploits our normal tendency toward "consistency-building" to help build tension, by designing into his work elements that undermine a simple, unified account.[6] Thus, we might view the contrary values manifested in the *Madonna* as obstacles to consistency-building. By this means Munch increases the intensity of his image and confronts us forcefully with actual conditions of our history.

This consideration begins to reveal why we regard the distinction between intuition and discursive reason as overdrawn. Langer herself is uneasy that the concept of intuition may open the door to irrationality and mysticism, and she should be. We argued in Chapter Two that the directness of symbols obscures the role played by the background culture, and we begin to see another facet of this theme if we add Iser's concept of consistency-building to our emerging view of cultural interpretation. We may now begin to take cognizance of the directness of symbols without losing sight of their historical derivation. Munch's painting benefits from its compressed allusions to historical meanings.

We can see it as an intelligent response to a history which includes the persecution of the adulteress alongside the exaltation of the mother figure, a history reverberating with the conflicting myths of Eve and the Virgin Mary. Munch's painting reveals diverse strands of that history by his violation of our desire for consistency-building. Although this knowledge is not presented in discrete logical steps, it implies no radical distinction between artistic understanding and discursive understanding.

If we are to develop an adequate understanding of the historical derivation of art works, we must develop rational principles which explain how innovations emerge naturally from existing cultural conditions. At first it may seem as if an artist like Munch takes a creative leap, which is discontinuous with his historical context. It may appear that something uncanny has occurred, something untranslatable into the terms of sequential historical change. The historical antecedents do not seem to account for the unique vision he created, but if we think of historical innovation in other terms, we may get a different result. Our strategy will be to approach it from the vantage point of visual languages, with innovations in pictorial culture being conceived as analogous to changes in linguistic expression.

In order to begin giving substance to this analogy, we must consider the apparent directness of our visual perceptions, and show how they would be construed within the idea of a visual language. We have already seen how directness of expression is to be understood according to the model of facial expressions and nonverbal communication, which depend upon familiar practices and routes of interpretation. A cat, for example, may communicate her wish for food silently, by placing herself strategically near her dish when a member of the family passes by. How are we to understand perception, viewed in light of these considerations?

For one thing, the cat takes advantage of habitual patterns in family behavior to communicate her desire for food, yet the family members may never consciously note the presence of these structures when they respond to her appeal. The apparent directness of response obscures the presence of general structures standing behind it. Similarly, Rudolph Arnheim has demonstrated salient features which enter into our perception of art works without our notice. For example, he shows how visual centering around a perceiver's body, the pull of gravity, and the framing of boundaries within perceptual space are factors in great paintings and architectural works. Equally, vertical and horizontal subdivisions, the arrangement of images along the diagonals, and other unseen spatial divisions enter into what we see directly when we observe a picture.[7] Rather than these factors requiring that we postulate a special intuitive faculty to explain them, they point toward the spontaneous role of cognitive elements in all experience.

Similarly, Gombrich rejects theories of perception grounded on the givenness of qualitative contents. He argues that "without some starting point, some initial schema, we could never get hold of the flux of experience. Without categories, we could not sort out our impressions."[8] Categories help to establish perceptual expectations, enabling us to pick out significant content. If our expectations are violated, we must either adjust our schematic framework or find a way to fit the aberrant occurrence into existing categories. This idea of a perceptual schema is illustrated by an appeal to Wittgenstein's well-known example of the *Duck-Rabbit* figure.[9] (Figure 9) A spontaneous shift of aspect yields a new perceptual whole; thus, the figure may be seen first *as* a rabbit and then *as* a duck, with no process of inference intervening. This difference of perception occurs without a change of line, since the same lines may take on either aspect.

Although this example may be regarded by some as a special case, when we turn to works of art, what is at issue for Gombrich becomes clear. Gombrich believes that the logical principles governing spatial organization help to determine visual content for the viewer. *What* is seen depends upon the method of projection. The skillful artist makes use of such projective techniques in communicating an intended meaning. This is one of the features entering into our idea of visual language. Gombrich associates the creativity of the artist with the modification of inherited visual schemata.

Let us consider an example to clarify Gombrich's interpretation. Picasso's *Les Demoiselles d'Avignon* (Figure 10) is a landmark painting in the development of modern art. It shocked Picasso's contemporaries because it represented an apparent sharp break with historical tradition. We now see it as foreshadowing the development of Cubism, and other new twentieth century styles. For his contemporaries, however, its innovations were severe. We should consider some specific points that will highlight Picasso's creative breakthrough. For example Picasso forms the curves of the women's bodies and the folds of the drapes by sharp-edged geometric shapes. He flattens the figures into the plane of the two-

Fig. 9 *Duck-Rabbit*
Reprinted from Norwood Russell Hanson, *Perception and Discovery* (1969),
Courtesy of Freeman, Cooper & Company, San Francisco.

dimensional surface, rejecting most of the conventions of illusionistic
perspective. Modelling the figures with the sculptor's sensibility, he
draws attention to the interacton of planes. He employs exaggerated
color contrasts to break up the surface of the flesh, and produces
dissonance in the image by giving two of the women heads modelled
after African sculptural forms, as well as by mixing frontal and profile
vantage points in the same figure. The figures of the women and the still-
life props are distorted in a variety of other ways. Picasso's creative
genius is prominently displayed in his radical break from pictorial
traditions. Or so it seems.

　　Gombrich's theory of schema modification points us in another
direction, toward the antecedents for Picasso's new style. If we examine
Cezanne's bather paintings, for example, we begin to see important
elements of Picasso's visual language already in use. Cezanne's large
Bathers (Figure 11, National Gallery, London), is a clear antecedent for
Picasso's work:[10] the bodily forms of Cezanne's bathers anticipate the
geometric composition employed in a more radical way by Picasso.

Fig. 10   Pablo Picasso, *Les Demoiselles d'Avignon* (1907)
Oil on canvas, 8'×7'8". Acquired through the Lillie P. Bliss Bequest, Collection,
The Museum of Modern Art, New York.

Fig. 11 Paul Cezanne, *Bathers* Oil on canvas, 51¼ × 76¾
Courtesy of the Trustees, The National Gallery, London.

Cezanne's figure modelling reflects sculptural ideas as much as does Picasso's, and his use of contrasting colors to form the flesh of the bathers, although more subtle than Picasso's, obeys the same visual principles. Cezanne's brushwork exhibits how images of solid objects may be constructed out of planes of color, applied in varied ways, and Cezanne binds the figures of the bathers to the two-dimensional surface, emphasizing the importance of interrelationships on that surface, in a fashion similar to the flatness we noted in Picasso's figures. Although there are other features common to the visual language of Cezanne and Picasso, we have said enough to reinforce Gombrich's idea of schema modification. We are interpreting Picasso's innovations in *Les Demoiselles d'Avignon* as modifications of visual forms which he inherited, and which remain as dynamic factors in his perception and in the development of his own distinctive style.[11] Not only Cezanne's forms, but those of artists like El Greco enter into the visual schemata Picasso employed. Although these antecedents do not *explain* Picasso's innovations, by linking them to the past in causal chains, they do establish a context of rational understanding indicating significant historical grounding for his work. We will have more to say in later chapters about how cultural explanation differs from causal accounts in the natural sciences.

One aspect of Picasso's originality in *Les Demoiselles d'Avignon* in his synthesis of Western visual traditions with the elements of African sculpture. Of course, he is not the first painter to make use of divergent traditions, if we think of the Tahitian paintings of Gauguin or of the influence of Oriental imagery on the Impressionists and Post-Impressionists. Picasso's synthesis of African masks with European painting is yet another illustration of what is implied by schema modification. He transforms the elements of the African masks, while concurrently transforming the imagery and concerns of the Western painting tradition. We should note, also, that he was not alone in attending to African sources, since Matisse, Derain, Modigliani, and others had similar interests; but they seem to exert a deeper hold on Picasso, perhaps because his native Spanish culture already reflected other African influences.

One important reservation about the concept of schema modification must be expressed at this point, before continuing our analysis of the visual language analogy. We may easily misconceive the idea of schema modification by thinking of the innovator as a relatively independent agent in affecting the modification; that is, we may think of the creator as a *projector* of schemata which would be another instance of the discredited idea of the creator as willful manipulator. When we think of Picasso's synthesis of African and European schemata, we need to remember Heidegger's idea that creation is "a drawing, as of water from a spring." The spring image reminds us that the hold of a visual tradition on an artist runs deep. Hence, the innovative activity cannot be detached from a context of symbolic meaning that helps to shape the content of the artist's experience.

We must remember also that our analysis has exposed the untenability of foundationalism, the philosophy of mind which views mental contents as the counterparts of objects, and treats symbols as mere complements of reality. We have reversed the usual way of conceiving the symbol-world relationship, holding that we can only encounter reality in terms of known cultural forms. This means, in some sense, that the artist modifies our *understanding* of what is real by changing the notion of reality he has inherited from the past. In this process, the artist is not independent of any and all cultural forms, but rather stands in a special relationship to them. We see this process at work if we consider Nietzsche's brilliant analysis of Greek tragedy. He sees the dramatist as undermining the concepts of human life held by the playwright's contemporaries. As Nietzsche sees it, the chorus plays the central role in this process: it generates an imaginative vision, within which the lives of the characters unfold; and it controls the interpretation of the vision by suggesting how the imagined occurrences fit into the lives of the members of the audience. This passage summarizes his view:

> . . . now we realize that the scene, complete with the action, was basically and originally thought of merely as a *vision*; the chorus is the only "reality" and generates the vision, speaking of it with the entire symbolism of dance, tone, and words.[12]

The chorus presents the vision to the audience and opposes its vision to the facile views entertained by the members of the audience before they encountered the drama. We are not to think of such visions as mere fantasy projections, but as ways of reordering our comprehension of the world from within. The artist's visions are not created in complete independence of the existing culture, but reflect imaginative expansions beyond the forms of comprehension already at hand.

Creative transformation is the concept we have been emphasizing from the beginning. Wallace Stevens has written a poem, "The Man with the Blue Guitar," which expresses this idea compellingly. The poem reminds one of the painting by Picasso, *The Old Guitarist* (Figure 12), from Picasso's blue period.

> The man bent over his guitar,
> A shearsman of sorts. The day was green.
>
> They said, "You have a blue guitar,
> You do not play things as they are."
>
> The man replied, "Things as they are
> Are changed upon the blue guitar."[13]

If the artist is capable of changing "things as they are" through the creation of imaginative visions, it is only because our comprehension of reality is relative to the limited perspectives already developed. Because our experience is symbolic through and through, we can never grasp reality *simpliciter*.

If we remember this interface between symbols and reality, then we have a better chance of avoiding pitfalls that attend Gombrich's idea of schema modification. We turn now to a further consideration of his idea that "the phrase the 'language of art' is more than a loose metaphor . . . ."[14] Visual schemata enter our experience without our noticing their presence, just as we use language without always being self-consciously aware of its syntax and semantics. We normally study grammar after we already know how to speak, and Gombrich believes there are analogous visual structures that are silently operative in our experience. One expression of this idea, offered by Winston Churchill (who was an amateur painter), is quoted with approval by Gombrich:

> We look at the object with an intent regard, then at the palette, and thirdly at the canvas. The canvas receives a message dispatched usually a few seconds before from the natural object. But it has come through a post office *en route*. It has been transmitted in code. It has been turned from light into paint. It reaches the canvas in a cryptogram. Not until it has been placed in its correct relation to everything else that is on the canvas can it be deciphered, is its meaning apparent, is it translated once again from mere pigment into light. And the light this time is not of Nature but of Art. [15]

Fig. 12   Pablo Picasso, *The Old Guitarist* (1903)
Oil on panel, 47-¾″×32-½″. Helen Birch Bartlett Memorial Collection, Courtesy
of The Art Institute of Chicago.

If we think, with Gombrich, of visual images as similar to cryptograms, we see the central role interpretations play in our visual experience. According to this view, even representational art fails to literally record features of the world, because it can only offer a coded equivalent for them.

We will understand this code only if we attend to the relationships the elements bear to each other. Gombrich's emphasis on the importance of *relationships* within the visual medium should be especially noted, since he believes that no element of the visual code has a privileged status in reflecting reality. Instead, these elements have meaning for us by lending themselves, as a whole, to a certain interpretation. Landscape paintings, for example, do not portray a particular place by elements in the painting corresponding one-to-one to items in physical space. Instead, a physical place may be portrayed for us because of a set of relationships that the elements of the painting bear to each other. Thus, it may be natural to interpret a stretch of blue color in the upper portion of a canvas as a representation of the sky, but we do not often enough notice how that interpretation depends on the placement of colors in relationship to the vertical and horizontal axes of the canvas. As Gombrich sees it, this "keyboard of relationships" determines the appropriateness of any given visual interpretation. He regards every artist as providing a selective schema of relationships in his work. He argues that the "artist will be attracted by motifs which can be rendered in his idiom. As he scans the landscape, the sights which can be matched successfully with the schemata he has learned to handle will leap forward as centers of attention."[16] Both the artist's perceptions and his rendering of a particular picture will be relative to his developed visual language. The relationships which take on prominence for a given artist will reflect visual structures of the tradition to which he belongs and elements of personal style he has already developed.

The emphasis on relationships is carried further by Gombrich's study of the role of teaching manuals in the sixteenth, seventeenth, and eighteenth centuries. He sees them as tools for training the aspiring artist in the syntax of his visual language. He points out that the aspiring artist was first trained in general forms of drawing, which he could then apply in making particular representations; these general schemata, of course, lent themselves to variations on the part of the individual artist. This phenomenon is not limited to the period of naturalistic representation. There are parallel contemporary examples, such as Alber's color guides.

Gombrich sees the functioning of these visual norms as an important ingredient in the development of the arts, since even inadequate schemata can be revised into more adequate forms, thereby promoting progress in the arts.

Although Gombrich's ideas about visual language are helpful in breaking us away from the intuitionist approach, we must be careful not to embrace his ideas uncritically. Before bringing some difficulties to the surface, we need to reflect briefly about the nature of language, since the way in which we understand language will play a large role in our assessment of Gombrich. It is easy to commit the same fallacies in our thinking about language as we have encountered in thinking about feelings and intuitions. If we think of languages as composed of individual words, with nouns naming items in the world, we are on the brink of the same confusions we have been working to overcome. Such a theory of language reflects a philosophy with the same inadequancies we have exposed, because it treats words as labels which abstractly characterize what has first been experienced concretely. Langer, for example, expresses this kind of approach when she says: "Intuition is, I think, the fundamental intellectual activity, which produces logical or semantical understanding."[17] Her statement treats semantical understanding, and language in general, as a second-order activity, built on the first-order foundation of immediate perception. Thus, complex meanings are treated as functions of simple, original meanings.

In contrast with this interpretation of language, Wittgenstein's *Philosophical Investigations* shows how meaning is tied to use. Words, like the tools we employ, have multiple uses, and the complexity of meaning that words have reflects this variety of uses. Wittgenstein asks us to consider whether children learn language by being taught labels for individual objects, or in some other way. His answer is that they learn language through use, by gradually discovering how to apply locutionary strings to situations. The elements of contextual learning are phrases and sentences, rather than individual words. Although he does not deny that we learn labels for things, he believes labelling is a derivative activity. The child finds himself surrounded by linguistic practices whose uses and applications are initially mysterious. How is the transition carried out from this initial condition of ignorance to linguistic competence? Wittgenstein's suggestion is that we think of linguistic practices as games, and the learning of the language as the learning of games. Just as the child learns how to play a game without first having memorized the rule book, by undertaking actions and having inappropriate behavior corrected by others, so he learns language by engaging in verbal behavior and improving on it under the watchful eye of adults. Thus, linguistic facility begins to be developed by imitation of adult behavior and by the child gradually learning more appropriate linguistic behavior in the situations he encounters. It should be added that we can never expose the child to all of the possible life situations he may encounter, and the models for verbal behavior he has learned will go on being challenged by other speakers of the language, either by direct correction or by their puzzled response to his utterances.

The discernment of rule structures is, therefore, a gradual process, one which operates almost by osmosis. Although linguistic practices generate rules, the child first encounters the active use of the language and only later learns how to define the rules. Although he is surrounded by semantical interpretations from the beginning, rather than encountering the world in terms of "pure experience," his relationship to these semantical structures is vague and in need of clarification. To summarize this approach, Wittgenstein characterizes language in this way: " . . . to imagine a language means to imagine a form of life."[18] Forms of life do not obey static rule structures, but have their own impetus which evolves rules out of practices. Thus, any of us is capable of speaking English long before we have mastered the dictionary or grammar book, although these guides to usage may help us to conform more closely to the general linguistic practices of our community.

This account of language begins to open up questions for us about Gombrich's idea of schema modification. A crucial question for our purposes is: how do we conceive the relationship between schema modification by the individual artist and the community practices on which they are based? If we think of visual systems as formal systems, then we may be impressed by the variety of systems that are possible, and by our ability to project interpretations according to whatever method of projection we might decide to employ. Formalism has become a dominant critical theory to account for developments in modern art, since the variety of systems of visualization has multiplied in quantum fashion in this century. If we think in a certain way about language games, we may be tempted to think of them as activities we can take or leave, depending upon our momentary preference. Wittgenstein, however, does not think of language games in such a casual fashion. They are more than *tools* for living, since they enter into the practice of living in more substantial ways than tools, which exist outside us and which we can put aside when our projects are completed. Schema modification is not like putting on a new set of clothes, or selecting another tool from the tool box.

In order to delve more deeply into this aspect of our topic, we need to consider the question: what *kind* of systems are linguistic systems? The formalist alternative arises from out thinking of axiomatic structures as the prototype for visual languages. Although Wittgenstein once held such a view, he came to reject it in favor of a more organic conception of languages. While a language is not an ideal system of meaning, it serves as a set of modifiable practices that can respond in changing fashion to the situations of life. One primary means by which languages grow is through the creation of metaphors, which suggest new meanings from old ones. Wittgenstein holds that we understand natural languages better if we think of them as bodies of meaning with many suburbs, to which new suburbs may be added at any time. Where we have the need for a new set of meanings, as in the invention of a technical vocabulary, a new subregion of the language can be created. If meaning is tied to usage, we can understand how this is possible. Thus, the practices of a community are open to change by its members, although the methods of change recognized as legitimate by a given community may vary widely.

Where Gombrich stands on the relationship of visual schemata to community practices is never as clear as we would like it to be. Sometimes his view appears to dovetail neatly with this Wittgensteinian account of linguistic practices, but at others to diverge sharply from it. To clarify what is at issue, we need to examine the idea of visual languages more fully. There are obvious examples of historical schemata to help us explore this theme. The most obvious is the system of Renaissance perspective, which dominated Western painting until the advent of Impressionism. Gombrich's idea of the logical schema is most obviously illustrated by it. The Renaissance system may be regarded as the triumph of geometric logic. This facet of Renaissance perspective appears readily if we consider a work like Durer's *Draftsman Drawing a Reclining Nude* (Figure 13). Durer displays the schematizing practices of the artist for all to see. The rectangular working surface, subdivided by a vertical and horizontal grid, provides a network of equal spaces into which the artist may project his image of the model. This arrangement reflects the Renaissance practice of treating the two-dimensional surface as a window opening into the depth. The projection of lines and curves into three-

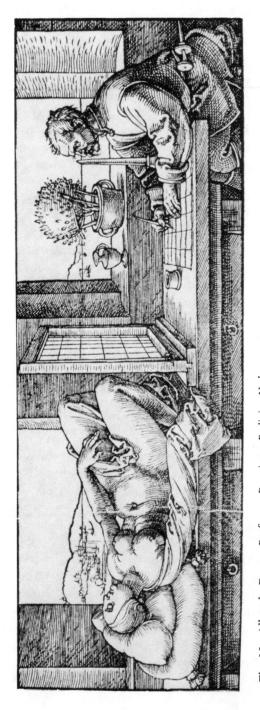

Fig. 13 Albrecht Durer, *Draftsman Drawing a Reclining Nude*
Woodcut from *Die Unterweisung Der Messung* (Manual of Measurement), Nurnberg (1538). Clarence Buckingham Collection.
Courtesy of the Art Institute, Chicago and Rosenthal Art Slides.

dimensional figures is controlled by careful management of parallel lines converging toward a vanishing point in the distance, with images of objects arranged along them in proportion to their size in normal vision. The different aspects of the model's figure are conveyed by lines and curves arranged according to these principles. The illusion of a real body in space conveys a sense of objectivity to the viewer.

We may regard this achievement of artistic objectivity and detachment as the triumph of method in visual representation, even as objectivity in science is achieved through method. We understand, as well, that other methods of projection are possible, some of which may express other artistic purposes. This consideration raises the question of how to regard the variability of visual systems, highlighted by Gombrich's idea of schema modification. Are they to be understood as variations in social practice (an approach bringing them into harmony with Wittgenstein's linguistic theory) or are they modifiable instead through the manipulation of structures, conceived in independence of their application? Gombrich's position sometimes offers support for one interpretation, sometimes for the other.

Suzi Gablik has, in fact, shown one of the ways to apply Gombrich's theory of pictorial schemata to create a formalist account of art. She presents a provocative thesis about stages of development in art history, which parallel stages of conceptual development in Piaget's psychology. She argues that the major historical eras (pre-Renaissance, Renaissance, and Modern) display traits strikingly similar to Piaget's developmental stages (pre-operational, concrete-operational, and formal-operational). Gablik employs some of Gombrich's own analysis to argue her thesis. She holds that pre-Renaissance art, like the pre-operational stage of intelligence, is simply unable to separate perceptual realilty from cognitive structure. This feature shows up especially in the spatial conventions, which treat space as an aggregate composed of solids and the void separating them. This topological conception of space is two-dimensional, finite, and concretely linked to the bodies which occupy it. Pictorial transitions depend on the grouping of things, narrative development being implied by the juxtaposition of images and repetition of elements within these groupings. In contrast, as we have just seen, Renaissance art distinguishes space from the *objects* that have their location within it. Space has been differentiated into an abstract network of relationships, infinite, and indifferent to the bodies it contains. Gablik holds that the geometric definition of space in the Renaissance tradition represents conceptual progress, the gain in abstraction permitting the artist to depict real motion and depth when fitting images to the coordinates of the picture plane. Nevertheless, it remains, she thinks, a stage of concrete operations, in contrast with the formal-operational thinking displayed in modern art, which frees itself from the static logic of a single, homogeneous system by emphasizing the dynamics of logical *processes*. These developments enable the modern artist to achieve autonomy in handling pictorial schemata thereby overcoming the inherent limitation to iconic representation in the Renaissance tradition. The gain in symbolic freedom, is she believes, the most important outcome of these historical changes.[19]

Gablik's approach helps us to crystallize an issue central for our understanding of Gombrich's concept of the visual schema. Changes of pictorial form, when conceived as Wittgensteinian forms of life, do not necessarily produce progressive development, but they may be regarded simply as changing practices useful in the conduct of life. Gablik, in contrast, has strong formalist leanings which make her regard modern art as the culmination of a progressive development. Here is her evaluation:

> What is both unique and exceptional in modern art is that the aesthetic impulse emerges to consciousness as *a thing on its own*; prior to the twentieth century, it seldom if ever stood alone but was always bound to magical, religious, or utilitarian functions. Nowhere do we find the construction of pure forms, or arrangements which are independent of content, within the history of art until after Cubism. Nowhere do we find an art based on pure propositional thought, *which is entirely abstract in intention*. Twentieth century culture, for the first time in history, produces artifacts which are relatively free constructions, made for purposes other than their concrete use: modern art is *art about art*, and about the intellectual activities of man . . . .[20]

In short, her thesis about the history of art reflects the formalist creed: art is now simply about art, and the artist's purpose is changed to the construction of pure form.

Although Gablik insists that her account of progress in art is independent of any judgment of aesthetic value,[21] her position raises additional issues to which we will return in later chapters. For the present, however, we welcome her stress on the hierarchical organization of the psyche, her grasp of the subtle interface between perceptual and conceptual processes, and her redefinition of the subject-object relationship in art. Although Gombrich himself does not endorse formalism, but seems even at times to oppose it, Gablik's development of his idea of visual schemata in the formalist direction demonstrates the need for a clearer account of how they are related to background social practices.

Meanwhile, the position being advocated in this chapter is specifically opposed to the formalist approach and to its attendant idea of artistic progress. For what reasons? First, formalism exaggerates the degree of autonomy possible within the creative process. This exaggeration results, in part, from its emphasis on "the construction of pure forms." Second, the freedom gained through abstraction threatens to undermine meaning by detaching visual forms from the larger context of life. As Merleau-Ponty has observed: "It is certainly right to condemn formalism, but it is ordinarily forgotten that its error is not that it esteems form too much, but that it esteems it so little that it detaches it from meaning."[22] The effect is to detach intelligence from it perceptual and cultural setting. Finally, purity of form appears to be an untenable idea, since it divorces visual form from its role in the interpretation of reality. Questions of applicability do not disappear with the death of Renaissance realism. The understanding of artistic intentions we have been developing points in another direction. That is why Wittgenstein's definition of meaning through use is so important for our later analysis. In addition to the objections to formalism already cited, we will discuss Gablik's commitment to the idea of historical progress in a later chapter.

Returning to our main theme, the creative alteration of visual languages can be conceived, after Wittgenstein, as the creation of "suburbs" resulting from new forms of use. In order to deepen our understanding of this aspect of the creative process, we return to our discussion of varieties of visual systems. So far the differentiation of Renaissance visual language from other forms has been presented primarily in terms of geometric-spatial concerns. However, even the Renaissance system included other significant elements, which will prove important for our later discussions. Renaissance artists featured the use of light and shade in figure modelling, thereby providing an illusion of volume. They emphasized anatomical accuracy in drawing, and they introduced the principle of "local color." These factors supplemented the system of perspective developed by Brunelleschi, Alberti, and others to form a whole system of visual realism.[23]

A painting such as Goya's *The Third of May, 1808*[24] (Figure 14) helps us to see these principles at work. Goya wants to present the reality of an execution to us, as an expression of the terror visited upon Madrid by Napoleon's troops. Renaissance pictorial conventions help him to conjure up the reality of the scene. We feel that we can walk into the space between the soldiers' guns and the victims of the massacre, because a perspective cone opens out between them, receding indefinitely into the distance, beyond the buildings visible in the background. This provides the axis around which the bodies of the soldiers and victims are organized, with the line of soldiers forming into continuously smaller figures to imply their distance from our vantage point. The light source on the ground illuminates the man at the center, with his arms upraised, while shadows are cast by it behind the soldiers. The light and his body posture make the man about to be shot the dramatic center of the painting. Local color principles are obeyed to some extent, with the dark red of a previous victim's blood staining the ground beneath his body, the color trailing off behind him. We could add detail to detail to illustrate the presence of Renaissance visual language in this painting. But we should also note that Goya's painting does not obey these principles in every respect, because we can see elements in his handling of color, for example, which anticipate Impressionist practices. Nevertheless, the dominance of the Renaissance system is evident in contrast with what we found in Picasso's *Les Demoiselles d'Avignon*.

When we shift to a radically different visual system, like the one governing Mimbres pottery, we see that the spatial conventions are different. The visual field in Figure 15 is dominated by the shape of the bowl, which is subdivided into four regions radiating from the center. Most of the designs on the pottery are variations on different kinds of symmetry (e.g. bilateral vs. radial symmetry). The designs are repeated, reversed, or undergo similar changes associated with different ways of turning the bowls.[25] This rotation system yields designs of elegant simplicity, most of them exhibiting abstract geometric forms.

Inherent rule structures which function as forms of life, like the rules of various language games, govern the activities of the Renaissance painter and the Mimbres potter. Other factors besides the space envisioned are involved in these visual structures. The function of the objects as bowls, for example, defines the visual field for the Mimbres potter. The materials employed, such as types of brushes, may play a role as well, as they certainly do in Chinese landscape painting. In the latter

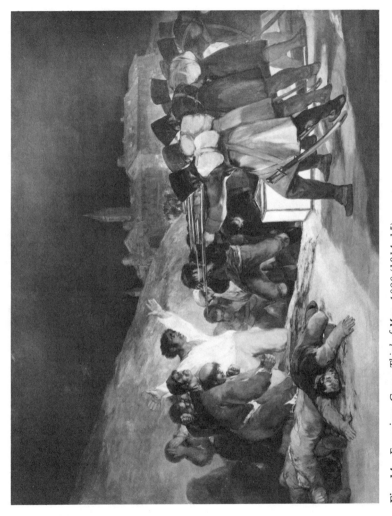

Fig. 14 Francisco Goya, *Third of May, 1808* (1814–15) Oil on Canvas, 8′9″ × 13′4″. Courtesy of the Prado Museum, Madrid.

Fig. 15 Mimbres Black-on-White Bowl, *Pair of Mountain Sheep Heads*
H: 4-⅛″; D: 9-¼″. Mattocks Site. Photograph: Justin Kerr. Originally published in
J.J. Brody, *Mimbres Pottery: Ancient Art of the American Southwest* (New York: Hudson
Hills Press 1983). Courtesy of Justin Kerr and the American Federation of
Arts.

case, we encounter a very sophisticated visual system, which diverges markedly from the two visual systems just considered. It lacks the perspective cone of Renaissance space, even though it reveals a landscape to us, and we find a different principle at work than the Renaissance window into the depth. We may enter the visual space at any point, and wander through it meditatively. The intricate, fine brushwork is definitive for the form of visualization. Instead of volumetric objects, whose texture makes it appear that we could grasp the objects in our hands, we are presented with delicate images whose form barely disturbs the space. The lines of a tree, for example, may simply frame the void against which they are painted. Conventions like cross-hatching lines are utilized to suggest the solidity of objects, but they are nearly transparent.[26]

These diverse visual systems make clear the role which interpretive principles play in the practices of artists. Twentieth century artists have, of course, stridently called this diversity to our attention. Elaborate experimentation with different forms of visualization has characterized the development of modern art. The results of this are obvious if we turn to a style such as abstract expressionism. If we examine a painting like Hans Hofmann's *The Golden Wall* (Figure 16) we see the developed results of a new visual language. The painting reminds us of Kandinsky's desire for the "music of painting." The elements of Hofmann's visual language are simply color and geometric form, abstracted from any reference to objects. Everything that happens in the painting, all the points of tension and countertension, are produced by color patches forming geometric edges. The entire work is explicitly a matter of relationships on the surface of the canvas, just as we saw this principle at work earlier in the paintings we considered by Picasso and Cezanne. Hofmann's work seems to display the principles of his syntactic structure in an open way. Like an elegant Bach fugue, its development is totally self-contained. *The Golden Wall* is replete with dynamic movement for the imaginative reader of its surface. For example, if one approaches the painting on the diagonal, beginning in the lower left corner, the slice of gold slides continuously through to the upper right corner, although it has been overpainted with other patches of color. Viewed as a flat surface, the painting provides the gold wall as the ground on which other colored forms appear. The tension produced by the diagonal, which pulls toward the background, and the utter flatness of the uniform gold, viewed frontally, is fundamental to the dynamics of the painting. The double

Fig. 16   Hans Hofmann, *The Golden Wall* (1961). Oil on canvas, 60″ X 72-¼.″ Mr. and Mrs. Frank G. Logan, Courtesy of The Art Institute of Chicago.

The large rectangle in the lower left is golden; this color pervades the background of the entire painting, showing through the overpainting wherever it is thin. (The dominant overpainting, center and right, is vibrant red in different thicknesses.)

The two blue rectangles referred to in the text are: (1) the narrow, dark rectangle to the right of center—just above and below this figure the golden color shows through almost without overpainting and (2) the uppermost rectangle, left of center and slightly above the diagonal. The sky blue patches referred to in the text are: (1) a small rectangle right of center and seemingly cut off at the bottom edge; and (2) the small section of a rectangle covered over by the golden rectangle in the lower left, and; (3) a few small patches peeking out elsewhere in the painting.

significance of the gold color, analogous to the tension present in an expressive metaphor, reflects an important principle of Hofmann's visual language, and of the language of modern art in general. Here is his own interpretation:

> Depth, in a pictorial, plastic sense, is not created by the arrangement of objects one after another toward a vanishing point, in the sense of the Renaissance perspective, but on the contrary (and in absolute denial of this doctrine) by the creation of forces in the sense of *push and pull*. Nor is depth created by tonal graduation—(another doctrine of the academician which, at its culmination, degraded the use of color to a mere function of expressing dark and light).[27]

The gold color exhibits Hofmann's principle of push and pull. The feeling of depth created by this, and other means, is created without the usual techniques of the Renaissance perspective system. The color regions themselves are utilizied as the elements which create this sense of depth. The creation of depth by the push-pull principle is evident from the placement of the two blue rectangles seen on either side of the vertical axis. Their relative postions and size make it possible for the active viewer to experience their alternate advancement and recession in the painting. Viewed as individual forms against their background, they appear to be just free-floating forms, but if we view them in relation to each other, beginning from the diagonal of the large blue rectangle, the space below it and to the right side of it recedes dramatically. This vantage point enables us to set up a figure-ground relationship where the one rectangle moves back while the other moves forward—push and pull.

The placement of the edges of the colored rectangles is ingeniously managed to produce a counterpoint of forms which add to this sense of depth. The edge of the gold rectangle in the lower left is related to the blue and green rectangles above in such a way that is suggests, again, the possibility of depth space. We can see also that Hofmann's management of the small pale blue color patches may be suggestive of the unlimited depth of the sky, as it shows through openings created by the other forms. The whole painting is a remarkable *tour de force* of color and form management. Planes of color have taken on the traditional unifying function played by lines in earlier styles of painting. The combination of the unified field of the painting with the pulsating energy it creates reminds us of the intricate relationships that enter into the finely crafted symphony. There is a sense of rhythm, of controlled intensity, and of expressive range which reinforce this impression.

When we compare this work with Renaissance painting, we find striking differences between them which may be regarded as reflecting alternative languages. Although there are points of contact between the two pictorial systems, the differences in conceptual approach are so fundamental that they are at least two quite different language games. Hofmann notes this difference of conceptual organization, when he discusses the importance of planes as the units of his painting:

> A line concept cannot control pictorial space absolutely. A line may flow freely in and out of space, but cannot independently create the phenomenon of *push and pull* necessary to plastic creation. *Push and pull* are expanding and contracting forces which are activated by carriers in visual motion. Planes are the most important carriers, lines and points less so. [28]

Hofmann's statement would not be valid, of course, if we thought of planes as composed of points and lines. However, if we begin with planes and view lines and points as constructed by abstraction from them, we get a different result. Thus, the intersection of two planes of color in *The Golden Wall* form a line at their edge.[29] This change of conception about space in painting dovetails neatly with changes in cosmology in science. There is a close fit between the visual principles of Renaissance art and the science which developed concurrently. Hofmann's spatial imagination reflects, in like manner, ideas about the relativity of space and creates a pictorial world which is more interior and more capable of opening out into the infinity of outer space than its predecessors. We feel that we can journey through his space without encountering tactile resistance. This is a noteworthy difference from the objects depicted within the Renaissance visual system.

These observations make it clear that Hofmann's freedom with visual forms is not necessarily an example of art about art. On the contrary, Hofmann's own statements, and his works, make clear his continuing concern to picture the world. Depth remains of prime significance for him, although he explores and displays it according to new conventions. It is defined by new assumptions, having to do with *surfaces* rather than with objects. As Krauss observed concerning Rodin, Hofmann endorses the "manifest intelligibility of surfaces." Or alternatively, we have argued that *forces* replace *objects* in his works. Therefore, we find Hofmann expressing a different world view than the one shaped by the idea of static objects: a result, we may add, unsurprising in a twentieth century thinker.

These considerations also show why Gombrich's stance on the languages of art is so unsatisfying. It is harder to fault what he says than what he leaves unsaid. He argues, for example:

> In our response to expression no less than in our reading of representation, our expectations of possibilities and probabilities must come into play. Given such a keyboard of relationships, a matrix or scale that has intelligible dimensions of "more" or "less," there is perhaps no limit to the systems of forms that can be made the instrument of artistic expression in terms of equivalence.[30]

His emphasis on a system of relationships is all well and good, but we should note the emphasis on *equivalence* in the closing line.

Gombrich emphasizes the symbolic equivalence that visual schemata may have to the reality to which they refer. While we have seen how Hofmann retains references to real things in his abstract constructions, Gombrich's theme of symbolic equivalence is not quite the same thing. This is so because Gombrich treats the visual symbol as a relational projection, a sort of visual conjecture, which can still be judged by standards of accuracy of representation. Gombrich *does* differ from the formalist because he retains this emphasis on reference in his version of visual schemata. The variability of visual schemata is introduced by Gombrich under the influence of Karl Popper's philosophy of science, according to which scientific reasoning is a trial-and-error process of creating theoretical conjectures, which undergo an elimination process by testing against reality. Just as theoretical conjectures may fail reality tests (falsification), Gombrich believes that some visual schemata may fail to picture the reality they attempt to depict. This idea repeatedly surfaces in *Art and Illusion* in Gombrich's recurring use of the phrase "making and matching" to characterize the artist's activity. He also speaks often of "schema and correction." What this shows is that the Renaissance *ideal* of objective representation remains active in Gombrich's interpretation of art. The variety of symbolic modes recognized by Gombrich serve only to point to more or less adequate modes of representation. They continue to be subjected to the standard of matching reality accurately.

But we ask: with *what* is the symbol to be matched? Since the theme of the last two chapters has been that the *content* of experience entails the shaping influence of visual languages, the variability of visual forms implies a relativity of content deeply embedded in our understanding of the real. Thus, the "making and matching" theme is misleading, since the question of what is *real* is very much at issue when we invent new interpretive schemata. Visualization and interpretation are inextricably bound together.

It is just because we can no longer separate form from meaning that the artist's visual logic is of such importance to twentieth century thought. Paradoxically, artists such as Cezanne and Hofmann have succeeded in reestablishing our sense of solidarity with the world by means of abstraction. This abstraction was necessary only because a particular system of visualization had become dominant, a system that contributed to our seeing things only as objects, forming a static reality.

That whole *system* of visualization has been challenged by developments in modern art. An open sense of the complexity of reality, and of the factors which enter into our visualization of it, is conveyed by the variety of modes of picturing invented in modern art. While Gablik is right to call our attention to the operational logic at work in modern art, our understanding of that logic must be made more concrete. We must address the ways in which color surfaces interact to define concrete relations within the world, how they form themselves into spatial configurations, how they transform a gridwork into a medium for imaginative exploration, how they, in short, contribute to an integrated visualization of the world. What Cezanne's *Bathers* shows us is the sense of solidarity between man and world, even as Hofmann's abstract network of color surfaces has done. The creative process, understood in this way, does not eventuate in art *about* art. On the contrary, our modes of involvement with the things of the world has become the subject for dynamic redefinition in twentieth century thought. This way of understanding the creative process hearkens back to Heidegger's image of creation as the "drawing, as of water from a spring" rather than to the manipulation of form by an autonomous agent. In the next chapter we will extend this theme by further considering the relationship of the artist's interpretive concerns to his presence and involvement within the visible world.

CHAPTER FOUR

The Artist and the Visible World

When we ask about the meaning of modern art, our response may be shaped by alternatives which are too limited. Since the ideology of modern art renounces naturalistic representation, we may think we are compelled to regard it as the triumph of subjectivity. However, this simplistic shift, which reflects an outmoded philosophy of mind, is untenable in light of the analysis of the last two chapters. Since visual languages enter into both perception and pictorial creation, we cannot any longer divide the world between the objective and the subjective. The very definition of objective reality is under the influence of processes of interpretation, and these processes function as formative factors in experience. No innocent encounter with the world is possible, if that means an encounter devoid of meaning. Thus, inherited standards of meaning relativize our experience and thought. In response to this relativity of perspective, we must give up the idea that the creative act is the work of the single individual, and move toward the idea that the artist's creative activity is the transformation of established visual meanings. We view modern art, therefore, as a concerted effort to question past visual culture and to initiate new interpretive possibilities.

Unless we exercise care at this point in our inquiry, however, the idea of subjective intentions will return to haunt us in another form. We may conceive of the relativity of visual languages in a manner which perpetuates subjectivism in a collective form if we begin thinking of visual meaning as merely conventional. Formalism may be construed in this way, with groups of artists busying themselves with the invention of new systems of interpretation. While this overcomes the illusion that the artist can create *ex nihilo*, it still may result in art which is idiosyncratic and unintelligible outside a small circle of people. The great works of modern art do not, of course, suffer from these defects, since they are resonant with overtones of history and nature. If we are to understand them, and avoid the pitfalls of subjectivism and conventionalism, we must revise our understanding of human agency and reconsider our assumptions about the relationship of human beings to the world. Without considering these topics carefully, we will generate confusion for ourselves.

Such confusion is evident in the writings of Gombrich, whose idea of schema modification vacillates between subjective and objective descriptions. He employs the language of subjectivity when he writes about the artist's freedom to change existing visual schemata, and the language of objectivity when he emphasizes the matching of artistic creations against reality. Although his theory of perception links the individual's perceptions to the background culture, he nevertheless writes as if cultural schemata were completely external historical factors. This dissonant note in his theory results from his failure to question familiar assumptions about individual agency and objective reality. Thus, while the new perception theory calls for a different account of how the individual relates to the surrounding world, Gombrich never succeeds in formulating a clear account of it.

How can we overcome this deficiency in his approach? We have already developed the idea of visual languages in terms of Wittgenstein's understanding of linguistic practices, which ties meaning to use. This implies that linguistic and visual expression cannot be detached from the surrounding world. In the present chapter, we will extend this idea by considering the theory of expression developed by Merleau-Ponty in his later writings.[1] His account of human expression links linguistic and visual expression together, and shows how both are to be understood as forms of practice within the world. His approach helps us to see how the artist is related to the visible world, and to overcome the artificial distinction between representation and expression as goals for artistic work. We will also come to see how perspective relativity does not necessarily imply conventionalism.

To begin our analysis, we will consider Merleau-Ponty's understanding of language. He rejects the idea that we have a merely external relationship to language and that language is just a tool by which we express ourselves. The way language enters into our lives is more intimate than this. Words and linguistic rules are forms of practice, and not just devices to be manipulated at arm's length. Semantical structures function, he believes, as *generative* structures, which stimulate ongoing linguistic developments. Here is how he describes expressive speech:

> Expressive speech does not simply choose a sign for an already defined signification, as one goes to look for a hammer in order to drive a nail or for a claw to pull it out. It gropes around a significative intention which is not guided by any text, and which is precisely in the process of writing that text.[2]

Expressive speech is not the selection of a verbal tool for conveying already perceived meanings, but it grows out of generative structures from which the meanings are formulated in the first place. The development of a speech act, or of a written text, is an organic outgrowth from existing semantical structures, which help to make it possible. The expressive act, therefore, is not to be understood as the application of a clearly conceived set of rules to a new situation. Therefore, language "is much more like a sort of being than a means . . . "[3] It is one of our modes of existence in the world (cp. Wittgenstein's "form of life").

If we are internally related to language, then how is meaning determined? Merleau-Ponty follows Saussure in conceiving language as diacritical,[4] by which he means that the signs in a language gain their meaning by the oppositions they bear to each other. Thus, a language is a system of differences, and individual words have no meaning apart from the relationship they have to other terms in the language. In other words, Merleau-Ponty rejects theories of language which interpret signs primarily in denotational terms. Where an interpreter like Bertrand Russell gives first priority in his theory of meaning to nouns, which name objects, Merleau-Ponty believes that signs have no meaning apart from the whole of language. While we may learn words in association with their application to things, their meaning does not necessarily consist in their serving as labels for things. Accordingly, our ability to experience and to think is made relative to language systems, because the network of meanings they form make experience and thought possible. For example, if we describe the flowers in a perennial border as blue, red, yellow, orange, and white, the force of these descriptions depends on the oppositions between the color words in English. We may only be able to identify color differences in the flowers when we have acquired the scale of differences from language.[5] The same thing holds if we describe them as lilies, phlox, hollyhocks, poppies, or delphiniums. None of them can be identified independently of established verbal contrasts in the language. Of course, it is not necessary that we know all the flower categories before we can apply any of them, but some internal differentiation is considered necessary according to the diacritical theory.

This idea gives added force to the claim that language is a kind of being, since it makes clear that linguistic practices are more than the application of abstract signs to objects encountered independently of the signs. The diacritical theory holds that we cannot detach our understanding of the kinds of things populating the world from the linguistic meanings we use to describe them. Language is described by Merleau-Ponty as a form of being, then, because of its formative impact on human experience. A part of what the diacritical theory shows us is how deeply indebted our experiences are to intersubjective forms of meaning. The linguistic practices of the community become the focal points for our gaining self understanding, rather than our developing it by attending to subjective experiences. Language is one of the primary ways in which our lives are linked to other members of the community, and the chief way in which community practices perpetuate themselves. Language is reflexive—since the verbal categories that I employ also get applied to me and my surroundings—and it, therefore, opens up possibilities of mutal expressiveness between people.

We can see this at work in the life of a child, who is encircled by language from the moment of birth. As Merleau-Ponty describes this phenomenon, the child begins by being surrounded by a baffling array of sounds, which mean nothing, and which gradually take on meaning because the linguistic practices of the people he hears are logically patterned. The patterns, however, are not self-evidently presented on the surface of the sounds, but they must be detected indirectly and gradually. When sufficient patterns begin to emerge for the child, this "sways the child over to the side of those who speak."[6] The original atmospheric nature of language is never changed, although the child can learn to take cognizance of elements in the atmosphere and how they function. Learning to detect the differences implicit in language, and learning how to apply them well, takes much experience and practice.

Because language presents itself to us as a form of being, we are unable to identify original elements of it which are more fundamental than other elements. Nothing is foundational in our encounter with language, and it can only be mastered in use:

> Only language as a whole enables one to understand how language draws the child to himself. . . . It is because the sign is diacritical from the outset, because it is composed and organized in terms of itself, that it has an interior and ends up laying a claim to meaning.[7]

While this quotation, and the diacritical theory in general, may appear to be a form of linguistic idealism, it is not really so in Merleau-Ponty's case. In fact, his approach gives us a way to understand why the idea of the mind has such a compelling hold on our thinking. Our experiences appear to have an interior, since a perceiver appears to have private impressions not shared by others. For example, I may look at the poppies in my perennial border and say that they look orange to me, while you may say they look red. This discrepancy in descriptions, which may persist after prolonged discussion, and which cannot even be settled by an appeal to the dictionary, may make it appear that we must postulate a subjective "theater" where my orange color occurs, and another one where your red color occurs. However, we can understand this phenomenon without entertaining this exotic hypothesis. If we follow Merleau-Ponty in the idea that a sign "has an interior" because it falls within diacritical structures, then we may reinterpret the subjective differences as differences in *usage* between two speakers of the language, who understand the opposition between orange and red in a different fashion. Their personal differences in the matter of the poppies may be construed, therefore, as a function of different personal histories, without our having to postulate different minds. For example, one of them learned the usage of 'orange' as it applies to oranges, while the other learned a more flexible usage. It all becomes a question of meanings and the interiority of meanings within a linguistic system and within a personal history of usage. Although there may be disagreements of belief, which entail different factual claims, many problems of description concern the indefinite boundaries that terms may have. Linguistic terms do not have the same sharp boundaries that physical objects have.

Therefore, far from his being a linguistic idealist, Merleau-Ponty shows us how to dispense with the hypothesis of the mind. If the theory of the mind is modelled on linguistic acts, as Wilfrid Sellars has argued, then we may be able to shift our focus from the creative mind to the creative *person*.[8] Merleau-Ponty shows us how mentalism might be thoroughly overcome, when he argues:

> The meaning is not on the phrase like the butter on the bread, like a second layer of "psychic reality" spread over the sound: it is the totality of what is said, the integral of all the differentiations of the verbal chain; it is given with the words for those who have ears to hear.[9]

If we make it a point to think of linguistic experiences as *integral* developments of intersubjective meaning, then it is not even necessary to postulate a mind as the seat of thought. Since our thoughts are modelled on meaning, the apparent interiority of thought processes can be reconstrued as a function of the internal relationship of meanings to other meanings in the linguistic system, and differences of thought as deriving from differences in usage. The idea that meaning is an *integral* of the whole verbal matrix helps us toward an account of visual meaning which does not presuppose the subject-object dichotomy.

We can apply this idea to a painting already considered: Hofmann's *The Golden Wall*. We have already noted the fact that Hofmann conceived his painting as revealing depth by different means than the Renaissance system of depth. He emphasized the creation of depth from the relationships between forms and colors on the picture surface. If we look at the surface alone, even when we feature the idea of relationships on the surface, we may forget that a sophisticated theory of visual meaning lies behind what is expressed. The temptation is to forget that whatever energy the painting conveys to a viewer is integral to the diacritical oppositions that Hofmann employs; e.g., the opposition between the two blue rectangles. Thus, the diacritical theory helps us to see that visual oppositions can create meaning, not like a "second layer of 'psychic reality' spread over" the forms, but as the integral of the visual differences presented on the surface. Therefore, if we follow Krauss' idea that Rodin stops us at the surface with his work, or extend this notion to all of modern art, we must remember that the surface is a charged surface, and should by no means be regarded as mere canvas and pigment, nor even as an exhibition of pure form. It can be abstract without lacking a matrix of meaning. The expressive power of a painting such as Hofmann's *The Golden Wall* is precisely the kind of example we need to consider in developing our understanding of visual language further.

Merleau-Ponty draws close parallels between visual expression and verbal expression, formulating his understanding of both in terms of the diacritical theory. He criticizes Malraux for viewing modern art as "a return to subjectivity" even though he agrees that we should follow Malraux in renouncing the "objectivist prejudice." What he argues is that we need not choose between these two stances. What is the alternative? We get the clue to it when he adds, concerning Malraux: "Perhaps he has too swiftly abandoned the domain of the visible world."[10] He offers us the distinction between abandoning the objective world and abandoning the visible world. This is important to Merleau-Ponty because he believes we *inhabit* the visible world, instead of having it deployed before our consciousness as a collection of objects.[11] We exist among the things populating the visible landscape, and it envelops us within its space. If our consciousness develops from within the space it inhabits, then expressive art is not the opposite of an art oriented to visible things. It follows that representation of visible meaning is not absent from an abstract painting like Hofmann's *The Golden Wall*. We have already seen that our concepts of depth relationships in the visible world are central to the abstract landscapes he created.

Things become visible as we move about in the world. They are not objects arrayed before us. Nor are there given contents of experience, detached from the visible things. Because we have no privileged stance from which to observe them, but must discern what they are from a particular perspective, our understanding of visible things can only be relative and contingent. When we stress our habitation within the world, we see that so-called representational art is already perspectival. The system of Renaissance perspective is "only one of the ways man has invented for projecting a perceived world before him, and not a copy of that world."[12] We must add, however, that projection is the wrong concept for describing the intimate involvement of the artist with the visible world. We will do better to think of Renaissance perspective as a form of practice, which is one strategy the artist may follow in making things visible. We have no independent standard for the forms that count as good representations of the real things.

The idea that language is a form of being can now be connected to the idea of systems of visual meaning. The forms of visualization that we employ express our involvement with the visible world. The artist is included within the world he depicts, because visual meanings are reflexive, just as verbal meanings are. He is visible, even as the things of the world are visible to him. Because of this close involvement, we must develop a new concept of the creative act and take cognizance of how the "artist changes the world into paintings."[13] Although this may appear to be an overstatement, Merleau-Ponty wants us to come to terms with a view of the artist's relationship to the visible world in which the subject-object split is overcome. If we think of the artist's active transformation of physical materials (pigment, canvas, etc.) and of his modification of cultural structures, it is not so far-fetched to say that he "changes the world into paintings." Our shift from the creative mind to the creative person requires that we see the artist at work in his studio, or in nature. As Matisse has shown us in *The Red Studio*, the artist is encircled by his own past works, as well as the materials available in his studio, and we must include these factors when thinking of the artist's intentionality. The structures of intentionality governing the creative process exist *between* the artist and other people, and reflect their mutual involvement with the visible world and related cultural forms. In this sense, the artist's studio is not a place apart from the world, where cultural creations are made, but is more like the gardener's plot, which can only be cultivated within the physical world.

The idea of human agency is modified greatly if we concentrate on human involvement within the visible world and within the cultural world, instead of beginning from the idea of a mind set against the objective world. Let us consider a nonartistic example to clarify this relationship further. Consider a sailor, beating into the wind in his small yacht, surrounded by rolling waves, gusts of wind, and an ominous dark sky. He has a vivid sense of his embodiment within the world, and there is no spilt between him and his sailing world. With his hand on the tiller, he shifts his eyes from sail to horizon, adjusting his hand to the changing conditions of wind, water, and sky. The tiller must become an extension of his hand and arm, so the boat will respond immediately to perceived changes in the sea. If he is to keep his charted course, the mutual adjustment of hand, eye, boat, and sea is essential. The sailor joins his sensations and judgments together in a single act, which is his sensitive response to the world he participates in. As the boat meets the waves, he must feel its place and movement, guiding it by reactions that have become instincts. From previous experience at the helm, he is able to respond with gestures which spontaneously reflect the situation as it unfolds. He is an exemplar[14]of the world of the sea, and he knows it from the inside, as one of its members.

The sailor's acts are expressive responses to his actual embodied condition; he must be at once receptive and active, remaining alert to changes in the surrounding sea which might pose a danger for his boat. If the sailor approaches the sea with an attitude of domination, his journey is likely to end in disaster. In contrast to this approach, he must develop the course of his ship's movement as his response to possibilities left open by the sea, which will not sit still for him to move from point of origin to point of destination in a straight line.

In similar fashion, the artist must be responsive to whatever aspect of the world he features in his work. This is just as essential for him as it is for the sailor. The idea of creative receptivity is important in Merleau-Ponty's understanding of the artist.[15] Expressive power is the consequence of a cultivated response to the things of the world. For example, when he reports on Cezanne's complex method of preparing himself for his landscape paintings, Merleau-Ponty quotes Cezanne as follows: "The landscape thinks itself in me, and I am its consciousness."[16] Cezanne, according to this account, gave himself over fully to the place being studied, and his attention was dominated by what the subject of his painting demanded of him. His attitude is more meditative than manipulative, reflecting adjustments on his part which are analogous to the sailor's responses to the sea. As Merleau-Ponty sees it, human expression must be developed obliquely, and is to be distinguised from a process of merely getting out what is locked away in the mind of the artist. Expression is the cultivated product of an encounter with actual situations.[17]

When we look at a specific painting of Cezanne's, *Landscape Near Aix, The Plain of the Arc River* (Figure 17), we can see the results of this process. The surface of the painting reveals a vitality and intense involvement, bringing the scene alive for us. The trees which frame the background

Fig. 17   Paul Cezanne, *Landscape near Aix, the Plain of the Arc River* (1892–1895)
Oil on canvas, 31-⅝"×25-⅛". Acquired through the generosity of the Sarah
Mellon Scaife family, Courtesy of The Museum of Art, Carnegie Institute,
Pittsburgh.

terrain seem to be living forms rising from the soil, like the trees we have known from our own first-hand experience. Cezanne has brought the scene to life for us, and we readily jump to the conclusion that he is a kind of magician, who knows exactly how to trick our eyes by turning a few splotches of paint into a real scene from nature. When we observe more carefully, and notice how he has constructed the scene by subtle modulations of color (variations on blue, green, and ochre) and by brushstrokes applied in different directions and thicknesses (establishing a sense of visual texture), our amazement at his talent may grow. However, this response hides the oblique character of the creative process from our view. It contains more than the spontaneous outcome of an applied talent.

If we attend to Merleau-Ponty's report of Cezanne's preparation for painting, we get a different impression. This is what he says:

He would start by discovering the geological foundations of the landscape; then, according to Mme. Cezanne, he would halt and look at everything with widened eyes, "germinating" with the countryside. The task before him was, first to forget all he had ever learned from science and, second *through* these sciences to recapture the structure of the landscape as an emerging organism. To do this, all the partial views one catches sight of must be welded together; all that the eye's versatility disperses must be reunited. . . . [18]

Cezanne does not manage the painting from the outside, but through intense involvement with the landscape, which enables him to discover the nuances it contains. He is not a spectator who skillfully records his observations; he works to identify himself with the place. If we think only of the natural scene, and of Cezanne at the moment when he began to paint, we will miss the contribution of his preparation and also the role of inherited forms of visual meaning.

The painter, standing before the river valley, marshalls his vision of the landscape from his active involvement with its many aspects. We are told that Cezanne would stare for hours at a particular scene, struggling to discover the motif for his painting.[19] His meditation, quickened by his keen powers of observation, was guided by his search for the principle which would enable him to render the scene whole. How did he accomplish this? If we look at how he constructed the *Landscape Near Aix*, we have a good example of his understanding of visual balance. The green splotches of paint occur in rhythmic sequence, beginning from the ground in the lower right, moving across the tree line in the center, and dividing between an arc receding into the background and a spiral rising to the tree tops. This provides a unity to the painting which is at once spatial, rhythmic, and a function of color relationships. This interrupted ribbon of green contrasts with the blue-grey and ochre splotches, which help us to read sky, hillside, rooftops, and soil into the painting. The painting's various aspects are developed in such integral fashion that it seems like a total organism, whose parts depend upon each other. Thus, tree lines are defined by the counterpoint Cezanne established between rising, vertical trunks and the largely horizontal green brushstrokes, which we take to be leaves. The roof lines, emerging from the breaks in the leaves, are molded solidly into the valley. The expressive power gained by Cezanne reflects in large part the brilliant sense of constructive balance found in so many of his paintings. Yet each painting required him to improvise anew, in order to capture the world he sought to depict. He could only arrive at a new balance by tapping into the richness of the enveloping scene and discovering a mode of visual organization that would reveal it to our view.

His attempt to allow the landscape to register itself through his experience reminds us of the sailor's active involvement with the sea. Like the sailor, the painter brings the educated movement of eye and hand to bear on the scene opening out around him. The movements of his brush are spontaneous responses that result from his intense relationship to the visible space. The receptive aspect of the creative process does not, of course, negate his own visual mastery, any more than the sailor's spontaneous movements obscure the contribution his own sailing competence makes to his success. Each of them draws from past practices, just as the virtuoso pianist does when he plays with such apparent ease. They are all bearers of what Pierre Bourdieu calls "cultivated dispositions,"[20] which put them beyond naive experience. The sailor draws on past sailing practices in charting his course, and chart and compass enter as aids to the spontaneous decisions he makes. The better he prepares himself for his voyage, the more able he will be to respond intelligently to any crisis without having to ponder his decision. Similarly, Cezanne prepared himself for the determination of a motif by deriving elements of style from the Impressionists, and from classical painting as well. His own distinctive style, developed out of these sources, was available as a repertoire when he began to paint *The Landscape Near Aix*. Like the generative sources in language, which are simply available to the speaker for new speech acts, the generative sources of artistic expression lend support to the spontaneous creation of new works.

The artist's "cultivated dispositions" are like new organs, and they become forms of "natural" functioning after a time. Merleau-Ponty departs from the distinction between the natural and the cultural, and he emphasizes the embodiment of the human person and the active role bodily involvement plays in the creative process. This is how he describes it:

The painter "takes his body with him," says Valery. Indeed we cannot imagine how a *mind* could paint. It is by lending his body to the world that the artist changes the world into paintings. To understand these transubstantiations we must go back to the working, actual body—not the body as a chunk of space or a bundle of functions but that body which is an intertwining of vision and movement.[21]

Merleau-Ponty's emphasis upon the "working, actual body" requires us to think about the *human* body rather than a chunk of mere matter. In *The Visible and the Invisible* he employs the category *flesh* to distinguish his approach from crude forms of physicalism.[22] We have already noticed two features of the working body of the artist which are not reducible to anatomical and physiological description: his reflexive relationship to the visible world, which we have observed in Cezanne; and the formative power of visual practices for visual experience. Both considerations bring questions of value and meaning to bear on the bodily ground of the artist's work. While Merleau-Ponty's attempt to overcome the subject-object spilt requires, in some sense, the embodiment of the human within the visible world, there is no reduction of human reality to the terms of a crude materialistic description.

This is evident when he describes the artist's work as "guided and oriented" by the visible things, or as "a response to what the world, the past, and the completed works demanded."[23] Although he says that "we cannot imagine how a *mind* could paint," this statement does not mean that personal characteristics are to be denied, in favor of the limited characteristics referred to in the physical sciences. Nevertheless, our revised philosophy of mind requires us to think of humans as embodied entities, and of human activity as occurring within the space of the visible and tangible world. Insofar as interpreters of modern art have spoken in the fashion of Kandinsky, and have characterized painting as autonomous conceptual construction, they have provided a misleading account of creative activity which fails to give sufficient emphasis to human embodiment. Because of this, we underscore Merleau-Ponty's idea that "we cannot imagine how a *mind* could paint."

This is not because the mind needs a body in order to carry out the physical operations of painting, but because human persons are embodied entities in all respects. The substantial activity of painting includes the "intertwining of vision and movement" spoken of above. While a body is necessary to place pigment on canvas, it is even more essential for the artist's perception. The idea of the intertwining is more essential for Merleau-Ponty's version of embodiment than the idea that we need a physical vehicle to carry out our purposes.

Let us pause to consider this idea more fully, since it is essential to our inquiry about the artist's relationship to the surrounding world. We can deepen our understanding by considering some ideas on perception of James J. Gibson, whose ecological approach to perception dovetails neatly with what we have been discussing.[24] While most perception theorists have studied perception from a static vantage point, which freezes the observer's position at a particular point in space, Gibson frames his interpretation for the moving body.[25] The key to his approach is the idea that information is arrayed all around us in the light, and each act of perception is understood as the detection of a part of this wealth of information. Gibson's approach contrasts with theories of perception which speak as if perception were the mechanical registration of an image on the retina. Obviously a mechanical and passive account of perception is poorly fitted to our example of the sailor, because he actively scans the horizon for salient information. Just this kind of case is the basis for Gibson's dynamic approach. Nor does the idea of mechanical causation adequately convey the intense observations made by Cezanne. Gibson holds that unless we define perception from the vantage point of the moving body, we will fail to do justice to the flexible responses to myriad fragments of information that are central in human perception.

How are we to think of the perceptual process in this ecological approach? Gibson thinks of the body as a total perceptual system, rather than isolating attention on the stimulation of a few visual receptors. He says:

We can think of vision as a perceptual system, the brain being part of the system. The eye is also part of the system, since retinal inputs lead to ocular adjustments and then to altered retinal inputs, and so on. The process is circular, not a one-way transmission. The eye-head-brain-body system registers the invariants in the structure of ambient light. The eye is not a camera that forms and delivers an image, nor is the retina simply a keyboard that can be struck by fingers of light.[26]

Gibson's emphasis on the total perceptual system makes the person, rather than isolated organs of sense, the focal point for his perception theory. Perception is viewed as the total response of the "lived" body to its surroundings, and Gibson regards the information available to it as potentially unlimited.[27] One reason for this wealth of information is that bodies are nested into the environment, setting up complex relationships between the visible things and any perceiver. No static vantage point will suffice. For example, we cannot limit our attention to detached bodies, nor can we find any other atomic units from which to build a perceptual account. The nesting of bodies requires complex approaches to visual space, and Gibson believes we achieve this primarily by detecting changes against a background of invariant structures.[28]

If we think again about our sailor, how this works may be evident. As he scans the horizon before his boat, the movement of the waves is relatively uniform. He searches out signs of change in the wind by watching for variant ripples on the surface. A change in the surface structure of the sea is an important indicator to him of the adjustments he must make. We need not treat the perceptual invariants as if they were Platonic forms to see the force of this idea. *Relative* invariants are all that is required for an ecological account of perception, and they may depend in some way on existing meanings. Gibson believes that a wide range of invariant features play a role in human perception, and he thinks we have barely begun to identify them in studies of perception. An example of a relative invariant might be gravity, which so far as our experience on earth is concerned is completely general. Other kinds of examples follow readily. Gibson notes that the things we see make their appearance in the ambient light, which forms an atmosphere encompassing us. Within its illumination we derive information from such factors as surface and layout.[29] We have just seen how surface and layout enter into the sailor's experience. In Cezanne's preparation for his painting, a more technical approach to layout and surface was evident because of the attention he paid to geological structure. In ordinary perception such features are implicit and rarely identified.

Our idea of the visible world fits into this orientation to surface and layout. Indeed, Gibson observes that "the terrestrial world is mostly made of surfaces, not of bodies in space."[30] The gardener who cultivates his flowers is aware of this, at least implicitly, because the layout of his bed is governed by the desire to provide variations in color, texture, and height which will interest the eye. The control of surface layout is also of central concern to the sculptor, the architect, and other artists. These common visual principles, known implicitly in practice, are often overlooked in technical theories of perception, and thus perception tends to be seen in mechanical terms.

Gibson provides us with a useful summary of some enviromental invariants:

> . . . the characteristics of an environmental medium are that it affords respiration for breathing; it permits locomotion; it can be filled with illumination so as to permit vision; it allows detection of vibrations and detection of diffusing emanations; it is homogeneous; and finally, it has an absolute axis of reference, up and down. All these offerings of nature, these possibilities or opportunities, these *affordances* as I will call them, are invariant.[31]

These affording structures are essential in our relationship to the visible world. Thus, upright posture is an affording structure because it gives us the capacity to derive visual information at a distance, and it enables us to observe contours and movements against the horizon. Our mobility also affords perception, our movement toward the horizon adding informational possibilities and enabling us to adopt different perspectives. What Gibson calls "occluding surfaces" (surfaces which hide other surfaces from our view) play an important role in our movement through space, because what is hidden and what is open to our view will vary as we move about the terrain.

Merleau-Ponty's account of human embodiment is closely related to Gibson's theory of perceptual affordances and his emphasis on the importance of visual surfaces. Merleau-Ponty had also stressed the importance of the visual circuit which exists between the perceiver and the horizon. He held that the horizon remains a constant element in the visible world, even as we move toward it. Although the visual contour shifts when I walk toward the hills, or toward the shoreline, it is only the visual content which changes, and not the structure between me and the horizon. One reason for the reflexive character of vision is our mobility. We can shift our position between over-here and over-there, and these positions are interchangeable. While we have already spoken of the intertwining of vision and movement, there are other forms of inter-twining relevant to this reversibility of positon. My perspectives inter-twine with those of other perceivers to form one perceptual world, and to make discourse about the visible world possible. this means I must pay the price of being visible to others, even as I am able to move about and encounter other visible things. Both human and animal perspectives include me within their scope. While the horizon is one invariant of perception, so is my occupation of a visible place in looking toward it.[32]

The surfaces and layouts which appear within this intertwining structure provide information to the human perceiver. However, we must avoid thinking of information in a detached, intellectual way, or we will miss the force of this concept. In order to call attention to the intimate link of the human perceiver to the visible world, Merleau-Ponty described man as the *exemplar sensible*. We have already encountered this term when we described the sailor as an exemplar of his sailing world. His is a life exemplary of the world of the sea because his actions are geared to its demands and fitted to it changes. We may think of the fish as *of* the sea in a way the sailor is not; the fish has gills for breathing and a streamlined contour for easy movement through the water. However, this reasoning is misleading, because the sailor takes measures to fit his activity to water, wind, and boat; he adapts his body to the sea by joining it to the boat, and he gains a power of movement exceeding that of the fish in many respects. We are in the habit, perhaps, of thinking of our adaptive responses to the sea as alien, technical measures, but the conditions of the sea are not really alien, maladaptive conditions for the confirmed seaman. The idea that man is a sensible exemplar of his world reverses our usual way of thinking by emphasizing the ways in which he is naturally attuned to his surroundings.

In this view, human sensibilities are not divorced from the things sensed, as if the powers of sensibility were alien powers. We do not *spy* on the things we see, but they enter into our perception as naturally as the air enters into our lungs. Color, for example, is not just a quality of external things that our rather odd organs are able to detect. It is a natural feature of *our* world, and applies to us as well as to the things we see. Color is one of the invariant features of the surfaces of the visible world, and it helps us to detect useful information in our surroundings. The dominant role color plays in our experience is only possible because we are naturally attuned to color differences, a fact which is consistent with a diacritical interpretation of visual experience.

We may build on this notion and get a firmer hold on Merleau-Ponty's concept of man, the exemplar, if we take into consideration what he says about color. He holds that we do not grasp colors as simple, presented qualities, but each encounter with a color, such as red, "requires a focussing, however brief; it emerges from a less precise, more general redness, in which my gaze was caught, into which it sank, before—as we put it so aptly—*fixing* it."[33] The fixing of color occurs against the background of general color meanings, and this general scale enters into our ability to focus on a particular shade on a given occasion. We exist within the hold of color gradients that we cannot escape. (But we should ask why we would ever want to escape!) *This* is what attunes us to color in the visible world. Color is one of the primary invariant structures that provide visual meaning for us.

Its appearance as an invariant feature of experience may create a seeming conflict with the diacritical theory of meaning. We must be careful at this point if we are to avoid a misleading conclusion. While the diacritical theory relativizes color distinctions, making a contrast like red-green dependent on actual oppositions within a given language, the idea that color is an invariant perceptual feature seems to imply that color is a biological universal. If there are biological universals of any kind, we seem to have a return of foundationalism, contradicting the line of reasoning we have developed. Further examination shows how this is misleading. If we think of the blood red color in Munch's *Madonna*, that color identification depends on a more general concept of red; blood red is a particular shade within a scale of differences concerning 'reds'. In like manner, the concept of red reflects contrasts like red-green which fall within the general concept of color. When we fix the red of the *Madonna* as blood red, therefore, we carry out this identification relative to general meanings which make it possible. Thus, the perception of blood red is simultaneously particular and general.

Viewed in this way, color as a biological universal for man does not contradict the diacritical theory, since the process of color identification *requires* specific color contrasts. The actual identification of blood red depends upon both color as a *possibility* of experience and culturally defined color contrasts. Thus, the biological and the cultural intertwine in our experience to such a degree that we cannot conceive of their separation. The information arrayed in the ambient light includes color as a completely general feature (invariant) without color ever being available to us in a neutral, non-cultural way.

The invariant presence of color highlights one of the ways we cannot break the bond joining us to the visible world. Our visual experience intertwines with our sense of mobility, and it intertwines also with what we touch, with what we hear, with what we say, and with what we think. Man's integration with the surrounding world is complete: he is flesh. There are no separate channels of perception, but the various channels overlap, crisscross, and intermesh. Although there may be momentary discrepancies between them, as there may be momentary forms of dissonance within any one of them, we are predisposed to bring our experience toward unity. We must think of these sensible capacities as active powers if we are to comprehend Merleau-Ponty's idea of human embodiment.

If we think again of Cezanne's painting, we can see it as in-comparable evidence of our solidarity with the world. If we return to his *Bathers*, we notice how closely the figures of the human subjects are molded into the surrounding space. The painting's geometric structure is fashioned with no distinction between its application to the bathers' bodies and to the environment they fit in. The same is true of the elements of *The Landscape Near Aix*. The painting puts us into the imaginative space of the landscape, as if we were there, surrounded by the trees. Just as we inhabit the surrounding world, we seem moment-arily to inhabit the visual space of the Arc River Valley as Cezanne's guests.

The power of the painter, or of other artists, to reveal our intimate bonding to situations and places is present in abstract art as well. Gibson argues that we misunderstand the whole process of picturing if we think of Renaissance perspective as natural and other forms of visualization as artificial. We should think instead of all forms of pictorial activity as artificial in comparison with the "natural" perspective of everyday vision.[34] If we see that *all* painting is abstract, then the way is open to finding continuity between modern art and its naturalistic antecedents. He adds:

What they need to understand in order to find a common ground, I think, is how it is possible for an observer to see something from no point of observation as well as from a given point of observation, that is, from a *path* of observation as well as a *position*. What modern painters are trying to do, if they only knew it, is paint invariants. What should interest them is not abstractions, not concepts, not space, not motion, but invariants.[35]

Invariants may be seen as the subject matter of Hofmann's vibrantly colored paintings. Apart from his isolation of attention on color relationships, his painting may be seen in Gibson's terms in other respects. If we allow the overlapping rectangles to guide us on an imaginary journey through space, the colored edges form *paths* of movement. Hofmann is a painter of occluded surfaces, exposing the invariant role they play in our movement through the visible world. Gibson's idea that modern painters are painting perceptual and conceptual invariants is provocative. It explains the continuity modern artists have with Cezanne and that he has with his predecessors. Abstract art, viewed in this way, simply isolates our attention on invariants more directly than did traditional art.

If we consider another example from modern art, Mondrian's *Broadway Boogie Woogie* (Figure 18), we can reinforce this impression. Mondrian displays a flat circuit of small colored spaces, organized into a gridwork. The skillful placement of colored squares, and the staccato spaces which intervene between them, give us a sense of movement and tempo as we follow along its visual paths. The painting may be construed as a metphor for the bustling activity of Broadway, reminding us of taxicabs, neon lights, and the movement of the crowd. And it may also be seen as a metaphor for the development of a piece of jazz, which has a movement and rhythm analogous to Mondrian's painted marks. However, Gibson helps us to see a more perspicacious interpretation: the painting reveals invariants of our perceptual world. We can apply its abstract patterns in multiple ways because it speaks to the way we glean visual meaning from our surroundings. We might say that Mondrian addresses our human ecology, and reveals some of the principles of our visual involvement in the world. By eliminating references to the things which populate the world and take priority for our attention, Mondrian has exposed color differences and shapes as *elements* which enter into our identification of things. His gridwork organization of space, broken by

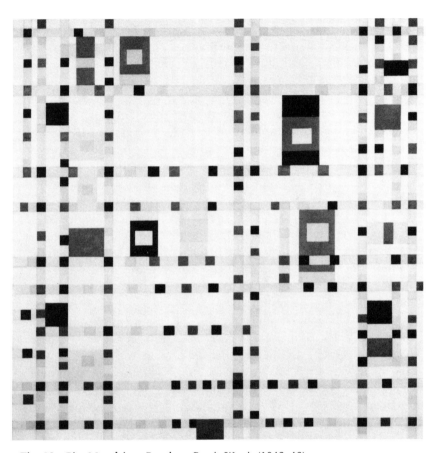

Fig. 18 Piet Mondrian, *Broadway Boogie Woogie* (1942–43)
Oil on canvas, 50″×50″. Given anonymously, Collection, The Museum of
Modern Art, New York.

the staccato movement of color, illustrates formal principles having to do with the very possibility of coherent experience. If we view abstract art in this way, we do not have to choose between an emphasis on its formalist interest and an interest in the visible world.

Whether we think of Kandinsky's paintings or other types of modern art, we can see the applicability of Gibson's concept of painters painting the invariants. If we recall Krauss' claim that Rodin stops us at the surface with his sculpture, we must be careful not to detach surfaces from the layouts of the visible world. Rodin's sculpture, *The Thinker* (Figure 19), which sits at the top of the gate in his *Gates of Hell*, illustrates this point forcefully, because his thinker shows us how thought is embodied in the world. If philosophers had attended to such examples, instead of isolating thought into a subjective theater, the theory of the mind would never have been invented. Rodin reveals a thinker at work in the world, with his chin resting on his hand as he ponders the significance of his life. His bodily posture reflects his absorption in thought and is in accord with our understanding of Wittgenstein's account of faces, gestures, and bodily postures. How else would we know that someone is in thought, except in the terms incorporated by Rodin? If Rodin stops us at the surface, it is because all art involves the skillful use of surfaces, translating human understanding into the terms of paint and canvas, or granite and bronze.

A distinction drawn by John F. A. Taylor helps to support this argument. Taylor distinguishes between the primary and the secondary image in a work of art, holding that the primary image occurs on the immediate, expressive surface, such as the two-dimensional surface of a painting. Cezanne's *Bathers*, for example, has as its primary image a certain arrangement of colors and shapes which charge the surface with energy. We may attend to those forms, without concentrating at all on the references the painting contains to bathers' bodies, trees, and clouds. These latter features form the secondary image, which is the only one the inexperienced observer of paintings notices. Taylor holds that the image of the bathers in the woods is secondary, and has always been secondary in painting. Thus, he argues that the shift to the primary image in modern art does not represent a severe break with the past. It brings to our attention what has always been central for the painter.[36] We have already seen how Rembrandt's *Old Man* may be approached in terms of subtle variations on brown, and this principle has been applied in

Fig. 19 Auguste Rodin, *The Thinker* (1880)
Bronze, 76" × 51-¼" × 55-¼", Gift of Jules E. Mastbaum, Courtesy of the Rodin
Museum, Philadelphia.

strident ways by twentieth century artists, self-conscious of their role as painters.

If this line of argument is sound, then the attention to surfaces by modern artists is not a distinguishing trait, even though so much pride has been invested in being modern. The role of the modern artist is not completely new. He shares with past artists the desire to make visible what might otherwise escape our notice. Cezanne's frequent returns to Mt. Saint Victoire to paint it again and again is symptomatic of the inexhaustible richness of the visible world, and of our need to have it presented anew. The artist's active interrogation of the visible world contributes insight and understanding to those of us who study his works. Since a variety of perspectives is always possible as we move through the visible world, the number of expressive paintings that might be created is without apparent limit.[37]

Merleau-Ponty's analysis of man's relationship to the visible world helps us to see that the artist's expressive powers are integral to his existence within the world. Thus, the subjectivist account of expression is completely overcome, and we can think about modern art in new terms. Merleau-Ponty's insistence that we think in terms of our embodiment shifts the focus of expression from the mind to eye and hand:

> The eye is an instrument which moves itself, a means which invents its own ends; it is *that which* has been moved by some impact of the world, which it then restores to the visible through the offices of an agile hand.[38]

Merleau-Ponty's approach gives us a way to overcome all vestiges of the subject-object split, and it also foreshadows an alternative to conventionalism. If we are to understand visual expression in terms of visual languages, the variety of possible visual forms is not subject to arbitrary invention if the visible world remains as the guide. Thus, even Mondrian's abstract compositions may be seen as responses to the invariant structures of the visible world, rather than just another formal invention.

We should not make the mistake of thinking that Merleau-Ponty has simply changed our understanding of the human mind. We noted at the beginning of the chapter that Gombrich failed to reconstruct our undertanding of the objective world. The analysis of the intervening pages shows us an alternative to the modern scientific understanding of the physical world. Merleau-Ponty could not have developed his account of the expressive powers of the human body without questioning familiar assumptions about bodies in space. Whitehead has argued in *Science and the Modern World* that the mind-body problem is traceable to mistaking mathematical abstractions for the very reality they are designed to interpret. He argues that the scientific view of bodies is modelled on operations of measurement, so that a body is actually conceived in science as the x which is measurable. This is one reason why Descartes felt constrained to postulate the mind as a separate substance, since so many human traits are not apparently reducible to the measurable forms of physics. We have seen that a conception of human embodiment as flesh, and a theory of perception which does justice to our depth involvement in the world, can obviate the need for a dualistic interpretation.

Merleau-Ponty has argued, in fact, that even physical dimensions have been misunderstood because of the highly abstract approach of modern physics. He argues that the controlling conception of depth has been thoroughly inadequate, since depth was treated as the third dimension, to be constructed from the two dimensions which occur in geometric theory. Thus, the body has been geometrized by modern physics, and our depth involvement in the visible world has been obscured. In contrast, Meleau-Ponty argues that our being in the world is characterized by many dimensions, including those of color, texture, polarity, and upright orientation. Thus, we must see human embodiment as polydimensional, rather than limiting our view to the geometrical dimensions so influtential in modern physics.[39]

These observations about the physical body, and its polydimesional involvement in the world, make it clear that we should not begin our thinking from the objective world of modern physics. The relationship of the human body to its surrounding space is active, dynamic, and temporally ordered as well. The dynamics of movement is captured convincingly in a charcoal drawing by Boccioni, called *Muscular Dynamism* (Figure 20). Boccioni provides an image which illustrates Merleau-Ponty's emphasis on how we inhabit the visible world. Expression is not, from this vantage point, an external feature of human life, but humans are naturally expressive: "All perception, all action which presupposes it, and in short every human use of the body is already *primordial expression*."[40]

These expressive powers are brought to a high state of development in the arts. If we think of human beings as naturally expressive, then the

Fig. 20   Umberto Boccioni, *Muscular Dynamism* (1913)
Chalk and charcoal, 34″ × 23¼″. Collection, The Museum of Modern Art, New York.

artist's style is of special importance. In contrast with a view of style as the external means for conveying the artist's intentions, Merleau-Ponty views it as an integral development of forms of visual meaning. His way of thinking about the artist is captured in the following passage:

> The painter's vision is not a view upon the *outside*, a merely "physical-optical" relation with the world. The world no longer stands before him through representation; rather it is the painter to whom the things of the world give birth by a sort of concentration or coming to itself of the visible.[41]

The way is prepared for this "coming to itself of the visible" by the development of culture. Now that we have clarified the relationship of the artist to the visible world, we must return to the subject of culture in its visual aspect. This will enable us to offer an improved account of the creative act.

CHAPTER FIVE

Meaning and Cultural Regularities

O ur understanding of human agen-
cy has been modified significantly by the analysis of the last three
chapters. The result is that we can no longer conceive of creative activity
apart from the artist's active involvement in the visible world, nor can we
separate his work from the visual meanings he shares with other people.
When Merleau-Ponty says that "it is the painter to whom the things of
the world give birth by a sort of concentration or coming to itself of the
visible," he is not simply calling our attention to a natural process that
takes place as readily as does respiration or walking through space. The
"coming to itself of the visible" can occur only in the presence of a
creative person, whose responses are the cultivated product of years of
training and practice. At the same time, we must avoid thinking of the
artist's activities as *unnatural*, as if acquired meanings and skills existed
externally to the human agent. On the contrary, they *become* a part of his
spontaneous response to visible things—even as the movements of the
sailor at the tiller do—because they have become integral to his life: like
all forms of cultural practice, the artist's activity depends on cultivated
dispositions entering into his experience to help make manifest what is
there. Therefore, we cannot separate nature from culture when we think
of the creative act.

Because the disclosure of any aspect of the visible world depends on meanings and practices shared with other people, we have come to regard the artist's intentions as a variant form of general intentionality structures. Instead of grounding the artist's work in his own mind, we have traced it to sources in his culture. Because of this, the immediacy of expressive works is deceiving, and tends to obscure the operative contribution that interpretive structures make to the work's impact. When we considered Matisse's painting *Dance* (Chapter II), we learned about the mediating role played by simple schematic forms. We have seen how skillfully Matisse stripped away irrelevant details, exposing elemental relationships to our eyes. By eliminating all but the most abstract features of dancers, hillside, and sky, Matisse confronts us with symbols of our involvement in the visible world, and of the culture we share with other people. While the naked dancers on the hillside speak to our participation in the natural world, the circling movement of their dance symbolizes our involvement in common cultural practices. In the present chapter, we will raise futher quesitons about the role cultural practices play in the creative process, giving special attention to the ways semantical structures determine visual meaning. Matisse's painting reminds us to attend both to visual structures which are evident, and to those whose absence may also shape our experience. In this chapter we will extend principles derived from Chapter IV, and will address questions about the relationship between nature and culture.

We have just explored the kind of solidarity existing between humans and the visible world, symbolized in Matisse's painting by the intertwining of the dancers with hillside and sky. Their fluid movement suggests how much they are at home in their surroundings. It suggests, as well, how much they feel at home with each other, as they engage in a common activity. The artist invokes the practice of dancing, with its overtones of shared folk culture, to display the joint solidarity of humans with their world and with each other.[1] The dancers symbolize the wider reality of shared cultural practices, collectively exhibiting what Gadamer describes as a "deep common accord,"[2] which spontaneously shapes their movements without always being consciously comprehended. Like the weather, the background of shared beliefs and practices contributes an atmosphere to what we do and think, even when we fail to notice its presence. These cultural structures are not even absent from reasoning, since practical reason, at least, is shaped spontaneously by them unless they are actively questioned.

We have seen how language is a spontaneous expressive medium for a human agent and how the functioning of language transcends the distinction we often draw between nature and culture. In substituting a semantical account of visual creation for a psychological account, we have been guided by the model of integral personal involvement we have in linguistic expression. This factor has been essential to our account of the utilization of visual languages, both by the artist and the perceiver of art works.

As a heuristic device this notion of visual languages has been innocent enough, and it had the virture of helping to wean us from an account of creativity that is too psychological. Nevertheless, we must note that, strictly speaking, visual culture is not a language, but is language-*like* in important respects.[3] Since complex philosophical issues arise when we try to specify in just what respects culture is like and unlike language, it would take us too far afield to discuss these questions here. For our purposes it is sufficient to see how fruitful the *comparison* is between language and culture for helping to reconstruct our view of the creative process on a nonpsychological basis. The whole thrust of the previous chapters has been to establish the creative agent as a person who utilizes forms of cultural meaning and practice, rather than our seeing creative work as stemming solely from a subjective source.

In thinking about the comparison between language and culture, it is easy to be misled by superficial differences, which divert us from understanding the ontology of culture. For example we are tempted to think that visual culture lacks rules, whereas languages obviously possess them. After all, it may be argued, grammar books show how speaking and writing is rule-guided, whereas painting lacks any structure of rules. We have already seen, however, that Gombrich treats the training manuals of the Renaissance tradition as counterexamples to this line of argument. Even though the training of modern artists normally occurs without such manuals, we may find other language-like elements entering into the training of today's aspiring artist. More telling than this point, however, is the fact that linguistic rules may not be so simple as the grammar book model would suggest. Joseph Margolis provides the right emphasis when he argues:

The fact is that although human language is distinctly rule-*like*, there is no reliable empirical evidence that there is a set of explicitly formulable rules that fit all the phenomena of intelligible speech *and* that are in some sense actually *used* by the speakers of a language. One can see the point very easily by considering that the meaning of any human utterance must depend on the extralinguistic context in which the utterance is produced, on background information and beliefs about the world that the speaker and hearer jointly possess. And if this is so for language, how much more certainly is it true, say, of period styles in dress and manners and painting and the like.[4]

Margolis' argument features two points crucial for our analysis: first, there may be functional rule-like structures in speech and hearing, although they may never have been formulated into explicit rules; and second, language in *use* depends on pragmatic factors not readily definable in a formal way. Moreover, it appears that the degree of attainable formality varies with the degree to which we restrict our purposes (as, for example, in technical, scientific studies). What this suggests is that the grammar book example abstracts from language in everyday use by focusing on the restrictive purpose of training people in correct usage. This may produce the illusion that the rule-structures are more central than they really are, even as formulated moral norms may give one the illusion that daily moral practices are rule-guided in a fundamental way. Margolis adds to our understanding of the normative aspect of language, when he says:

> . . . to say that language is rule-*like* is to say that there is a certain *intensional regularity* that informs the practice of speech, that cannot be fully formalized, that depends on context, and that is open to deliberate and accidental change over time. . . . There are no determinate universal rules (governing either language or other cultural phenomena) that linguistic ability presupposes; but there are more or less prevailing regularities that rough-and-ready rules of thumb or maxims (or more ambitiously, institutions, traditions, genres, styles, and the like) reasonably collect; and *these* may inform the causal agency of human persons.[5]

Since the informal regularities of language are more like rules of thumb than like formally codified laws, their functioning within language may not really differentiate them from cultural generalities. Let us consider the functioning of cultural generalities for a moment, in order to compare them further with language.

If we remember Munch's *Madonna*, a particular shade of red is central to the expressive content of the painted image. Yet the exact role played by this red in creating visual meaning is more complicated that it first appears. What we can see clearly from our earlier analysis is that the blood red of the background of the madonna figure gains its force, in part, from how it fits with the other colors in the painting. This much has been established by the diacritical theory of meaning discussed in Chapter IV. Moreover, this color is also relative to other reds appearing in a variety of settings within nature and in other paintings. Each of these reds is a *token* of a general type we know abstractly as red.[6] These tokens function as particular examples of the type, which may nevertheless lack definite boundaries. Accordingly, we may encounter debates about whether a particular color is an example of red or of some other color closely related to it. In a sense it is always a matter of judgment whether any given token exemplifies the general type to which it may be related in certain respects. If we follow Margolis' strategy in this matter, we must treat the determination of the boundaries of the type as a matter for adjudication by the members of a given cultural group. Although they all know the approximate range of color concepts, each new token may shift their understanding in unpredictable ways. This implies in general that the meaning of art works is always subject to contextual determination, since cultural entities exhibit and express open-textured properties.

In other words, although there are visual regularities, they are language-like in being informal and context-dependent. And also like linguistic regularities, they manifest themselves through a physical medium on which they depend, but with which they are not identical. This latter point is particularly clear from our discussions of color in the last chapter, since the biological capacity for color-discrimination only gets actualized by perceptual acts into which cultural distinctions enter. Although we think of the perception of red, for example, as the perception of a physical condition, the bodily state does not, in and of itself, fix the content of the perceptual experience. This is just because we have shown that the logical content of a concept like red is not fixed apart from culturally-based judgments. These considerations reveal the way in which nature and culture jointly contribute to human perception, making it difficult for us to separate them with respect to art works. Works of art are as physical as anything may be, but their cultural aspect includes regularities which can only be explained by attending to systems of meaning.

This theme of the integral relationship between nature and culture can be developed further by considering certain features of Roman Jakobson's linguistic theory. Since Jakobson advocates the diacritical theory of meaning, his analysis meshes readily with the treatment just given of cultural regularities. He cites two features essential for understanding linguistic phenomena: (1) they depend on physical differences, manifested as sound differences in the production and reception of speech (studied in phonetics and acoustics); and (2) they depend on what he calls *phonemic* differences, which presuppose sound differences without being identical with them. The phoneme is the linguistic element which represents the minimum *functional* unit by which we make linguistic discriminations. Phonemes are the object of phonological studies, which deal with linguistic differences that are manifested in linguistic practice.[7] While the phoneme is composed of a bundle of sound differences, which are complex patterns of change recorded and studied on acoustic instruments, phonemic differences concern differences we are able to *hear*, or differences perceived in practice.[8]

Jakobson holds, in fact, that phonemic elements are relative to a given linguistic tradition, different elements being significant in different linguistic groups. The same element may differ in its function from one language to another. For example Jakobson points out that stress varies in its function between Russian, Czech, and French, since it differentiates the meanings of words in Russian (by having its position varied), delimits words in Czech (because it has fixed position), and plays an emotive-expressive role in French.[9] This means that phonemes present the linguist with questions of *linguistic value*, because the student who wishes to avoid distorting linguistic practices must incorporate consideration of linguistic roles into his study.

When the phoneme is made a central element in linguistic studies, it is clear that both natural and cultural aspects come under scrutiny. Phonemes function as natural units insofar as they are bundles of sounds and as cultural units insofar as they reflect the conventional practices of a given social group. Jakobson holds that we cannot identify any phoneme apart from an established system of language, but he holds also that the phoneme as such lacks any value of its own. Thus, we might say that the phoneme is the natural basis for linguistic practice, even though we can identify it only within a given set of practices. Jakobson's stance on this matter is made clear when he asks:

... what value corresponds to the difference between two phonemes? What corresponds to the difference between two phonemes
is solely the *fact* of a difference in meaning, whereas the *content* of
these different meanings varies from one word to another.[10]

Although phonemic oppositions pattern our linguistic practice, helping
us to achieve sense discriminations with respect to what we say and hear,
they nevertheless lack any positive content of their own. They only gain
significance from the roles they play within a given linguistic system.
While they make actual sense discriminations possible, they have no
inherent significance apart form this practical function. This point is
especially important because the actualization of phonemic potentials
(which are, after all, merely natural differences) invariably involves
already constituted values. The broad significance of this point is not
missed by Jakobson, who observes:

> The ontological problem of what form of reality is concealed behind
> the idea of the phoneme is in fact not at all specific to the idea of the
> phoneme. It is actually one particular example of a much more
> general question: what kind of reality is to be attributed to linguistic
> values, or even to semiotic values in general?[11]

The general question about semiotic or cultural values is the central
question of this and the next chapter. What, in general, is the ontological
make-up of cultural works? And how are art works to be regarded within
a general account of reality?

Cultural studies very often turn into another form of nature study.
Jakobson himself objects to earlier linguistic studies for just this
tendency to stress motor and acoustic aspects of language without taking
into account a functional analysis. The tendency of cultural studies to
reduce culture to nature has been labelled the stratigraphic fallacy by
Clifford Geertz.[12] The stratigraphic approach to culture defines human
reality in terms of different levels, all of which are grounded on a basic
biological level. According to this approach, cultural reality is one of the
upper strata of human life, rooted in the biological, the psychological,
and the social structures which undergird it. Geertz's objection to the
stratigraphic approach, which may seem so uncontroversial within our
scientific world view, is that it treats culture as an add-on, instead of
recognizing its integral role in human existence. Contrary to this

"lowest-common-denominator view of humanity,"[13] Geertz aspires to an account of human reality emphasizing cultural forms as "webs of significance," thereby making anthropology "not an experimental science in search of law but an interpretive one in search of meaning."[14] This approach dovetails neatly with the nonfoundational account of experience we have developed and also with Jakobson's approach to the nature-culture question with respect to language. Accordingly, biology is to be regarded as no more foundational than culture is for man.

While Jakobson's approach to language makes this clear with respect to the functioning of the phoneme, he also makes it clear by the questions he poses about linguistic values. A reciprocal relationship between nature and culture is recognized if we accept phonemic oppositions as the natural basis for linguistic values, and linguistic practices as the context within which phonemic differences appear. While the phoneme makes other linguistic elements possible (words and phrases, for example), it can play this role only within an extant language system. Otherwise the phoneme is simply a physical difference lacking any significance. At the same time phonemic oppositions are the natural basis for attaining conventional meaning. Words, for example, are conventional signifiers capable of forming themselves into complex strings also having conventional meaning. Phonemes are understood by Jakobson as "non-decomposable *distinctive features*."[15] Although they may be acoustically complex, the bundle of sound features that each phoneme forms provides the basis for value discriminations that inevitably appear with words and phrases. Meaning develops, in this sense, out of sound. How this is possible becomes clear when we shift the example away from language to other kinds of values. Jakobson observes:

> Imagine three dollars, one of which is paper, and two are metal coins, one of which is worn and the other shining new. A child might set apart the worn coin from the new coin, and a numismatist might classify them according the the year in which they were coined. But for the community at large the three dollars all have the same fiduciary value.[16]

What this passage suggests is that values depend on perceived differences and on varied purposes. Thus, the physical differences between the coins can become the basis for the numismatist's scale of values to be applied, and for the child's as well. However, both cases bring specialized interests to bear on these differences, in contrast with the general community's exchange values which ignore them. Thus, for purposes of monetary exchange, they have the same value, although for the purposes of numismatist and child they do not.

The general conclusion to which these examples point is that all semiotic or cultural values depend on physical differences which take on conventional significance by being singled out for special uses. In this sense *any* physical difference might be made the basis of a valuational distinction, although it is clear that some differences are more naturally attuned to one use rather than another. Thus, it is unsurprising that sound differences have become the basis for linguistic value in speaking and hearing. If we extend Jakobson's concept of phonemic opposition to other kinds of differences, we see the force of these considerations. For example, a graphic language might be regarded as composed of graphemes, whose distinctive features make possible conventional visual values, which depend on them without the graphemes having inherent value of their own. Modes of visual expression develop in conjunction with the visual regularities resulting from these forms of visual signifi-cance. This is, in fact, the conception of visual languages that has been guiding our discussions in earlier chapters.

The significance of Jakobson's language theory for the arts can be made even clearer if we extend his account of the generation of linguistic meaning out of sound differences to develop an account of musical meaning. Phonemic oppositions occur in music as well, making it possible for performers and listeners to follow sound patterns according to the conventional regularities governing music. Notes, key signatures, rhythmic patterns, chord patterns, and the like are conventional refinements which transform phonemic differences into patterns of sound having musical value. In addition to these sound elements, a system of graphic notation has been superadded to guide performers in the reenactment of musical patterns. While the conventional system of Western music evolved from phonemic oppositions is remarkably complex and advanced in its possibilities for expression, the principles Jakobson reveals in his analysis of linguistic meaning seem to hold here as well. We can say, then, that musical culture is language-like in its make-up and in its potential for ongoing development.

In earlier chapters we argued both that Kandinsky's dream of the "music of painting" should be construed as his desire for a more highly developed visual language; and that the formalist understanding of art misconceived the nature of cultural regularities. We are now prepared to push these observations further. Because music has perhaps the most highly developed conventions of any of the arts, it appears to be closest to exemplifying rule-guided practices. For this reason formalism finds its most substantial support from music, with the composer apparently having autonomy in the handling of varied musical forms, independent of any direct referential limitations. Music, it appears, is simply about music, and may be regarded as wholly confined within musical "space."

According to this approach, the expressive power of music results from the free development of musical forms, conceived as a separate domain of culture. Music theory points toward such features as the diatonic scale, key signatures, major and minor modes, and basic harmonic and rhythmic relationships. The theory of how these elements are related in Western music is a sophisticated technical study. It forms the basis of the composer's creation of new musical works. The formalist treats musical forms as similar to syntactic structures, with new works being created by permutations and combinations governed by the rules of musical "grammar" alone. If we think of composition in these terms, then conventional structures such as the symphony represent traditional patterns available for the composer's consideration, and the content of new works result from variations he is able to conceive in these conventional forms. The distinctively musical concerns are served when the composer attends to musical forms alone, apart from extraneous concerns that may enter into the creation of his work.

This view of the formalist has both a strength and a serious weakness. Its strength is in recognizing the importance of the musical medium in musical expression. The concept of the medium deserves emphasis, because self-conscious attention to medium has played such a central role in the development of twentieth century art. It is no accident that formalism as a critical theory has developed in response to modern art. In music, modifications in the medium have been evident in the strident innovations of such modern composers as Schoenberg, Berg, and Stravinsky, and certain composers (e.g., John Cage) have made their music a self-conscious exemplification of a formalist understanding of the medium. Our emphasis on the development of meaning from sound might make it appear that we are viewing art simply as an extension of natural forms of expression, without taking the medium adequately into account.

In order to counterbalance this impression, we need to briefly consider the medium's contribution to the creative process. John Dewey, whose aesthetic theory is similar in many respects to the position being outlined here, has made important contributions to understanding the intrinsic importance of the artistic medium. Natural materials become transformed into a medium when they are isolated from their normal function and turned into "a mode of language."[17] Dewey illustrates this with some observations about color:

> In any ordinary perception, we see by means of light; we distinguish by means of reflected and refracted colors: that is a truism. But in ordinary perceptions, this medium of color is mixed, adulterated. While we see, we also hear; we feel pressures, and heat or cold. In a painting, color renders the scene without these alloys and impurities. They are part of the dross that is squeezed out and left behind in an act of intensified expression. The medium becomes color alone, and since color alone must now carry the qualities of movement, touch, sound, etc . . . the expressiveness and energy of color are enhanced.[18]

The intensification of color in painting, or of sound in music, results from an exclusive focus on them as elements. Even more importantly, Dewey shows that this isolation makes these materials into the artistic elements from which works are composed. He reports that Delacroix complained that his contemporary painters "used coloration rather than color," a remark which Dewey construes as meaning "that they applied color *to* their represented objects instead of making them out of color."[19] The formalist position has its greatest strength in the recognition it gives to the constructive use of the elements of the medium and to the variety of expressive possibilities this entails.

However, formalism's weakness rests in the abstraction of these constructive activities from the larger semantical context within which they fall—an error which Dewey does not make. While there are distinctive musical values, musical works express larger concerns of life as well. Just as visual languages provide us with ways of seeing, so musical languages may contribute frameworks for hearing which can alter the emotional responses we have to the conditions of our existence. The creations of individual composers and performers are capable of contributing growth to our understanding, and not just to the historical development of music itself. Accordingly, we treat musical "language" as an interpreted language, whose expressive potentional includes its relationship to larger emotional features of our lives. Even the musical genres that are seemingly most self-contained have meaning which goes beyond musical "space."[20]

If we are to make this idea count for anything, we must clarify precisely how musical structures may be regarded as semantic and pragmatic regularities. Let us consider Shostakovich's *Symphony No. 5*, which takes as its main theme the struggle of man to attain his ideals, amidst hostile conditions. From the opening bars of the symphony, Shostakovich evokes emotional conflict for the listener by a tension expressed within the strings.

The occasional dissonant tones he employs are reinforced by a clipped rhythm which invests the music with an unsettled emotional tone. Similarly, other voices of the orchestra reiterate the conflicts first heard in the strings, with both a basoon-oboe combination and a later combination of higher and lower brass mirroring this. Then follows the lofty, lyrical expression of human aspirations, when the smooth strains of the violin, set within a regular rhythmic pattern, create a contrast with the orchestral voices in the earlier sections. The two themes finally join together in the concluding section of the movement, producing a complex emotional context for the listener from these contrasting developments.

How are we to think of this description of Shostakovich's symphony, which takes the liberty of extending psychological terms to music? Is this a valid extension, or is it simply a failure on our part to understand the music as the musical purist would? We do not, of course, think that the violins, whose lyric theme is introduced by heralding trumpets, literally possess lofty ideals, nor that the sounds of hostility, conveyed largely by the cellos and double bass, are literally properties of these instruments. However, they are *expressive* of these emotional states, because the music is capable of conveying meaning beyond the mere presentation of sounds. An observation by Schopenhauer, quoted by Nietzsche, is appropriate in this connection:

... whoever gives himself up entirely to the impression of a symphony, seems to see all the possible events of life and the world take place in himself; yet if he reflects, he can find no likeness between the music and the things that passed before his mind.[21]

In other words, the power of music to express meanings depends on the *symbolic* power of music, rather than on any literal replication of the events of life in the music. If we speak, then, of music possessing semantical structures, it is not because music literally mirrors life, but because we can find applications through it to what is independently important. The whole force of the line of reasoning of the last three chapters is that psychological states, such as hostility, occur in conjunction with systems of meaning: faces and bodily gestures are expressive of such states, but so are pictures and musical works. Works of art are able to express human feeling in deeper ways than merely by association, because feelings are first born in the womb of cultural reality. Or rather, feelings and expressive forms are so intertwined that they form one reality in human experience.

This is why Shostakovich can evoke emotional conflicts through his music, for the history of our emotional development is intertwined with musical forms, even as it is with faces and tones of voice. The musical medium heightens the composer's expressive range because, as Suzanne Langer has argued, "sound is a negotiable medium," fitted to emplot patterns of development within our experience. Langer believes that this emplotment is possible because the logical patterns of sentience and the logical patterns of music are similar, leading her to describe music as "a tonal analogue of emotive life."[22] This is because the fluidity of sound in music permits it to serve both as a symbol for feeling and as a source capable of evoking feeling as a response.

This dual power of the musical medium reinforces our treatment of music as language-like. The ability of both music and language to symbolize and evoke meanings points toward their shared nature as semantic-pragmatic structures. They are both dependent on background beliefs and practices. Music's special power to convey emotional meaning may have its explanation in a claim made by Dewey: "Because of the connections of hearing with all parts of the organism, sound has more reverberations and resonances than any other sense."[23] Whether this is true or not, the close association between music and language lends credence to Dewey's further claim that "through the use of instruments, sound is freed from the definiteness it has acquired through speech. It thus reverts to its primitive passional quality. It achieves generality, detachment, from particular objects and events."[24] This view has the advantage over a formalist approach to music in that it recognizes the role of the musical medium without losing sight of important semantical functions it is able to play.

The composer, then, makes use of such factors as changes of tempo, contrasting tone qualities, rhythmic alterations, the reiteration and variation of themes, and patterns of intensification and release to give expressive force to his music. While many of these same factors enter into speech, the transformation of sound into a musical medium enhances the expressive power it contains in speech. A similar enhancement is produced within language itself by poetic structures. These considerations make it clear that no category mistake has been committed in our attributing emotional qualities and other personal qualities to the Shostakovich work.

The symphonic structure itself contributes to this enhanced power of expression. The dramatic tension of the first movement is released in the second, or scherzo movement, which conveys the playful, happy gestures of a carefree dance. This is only a temporary interlude, however, and the slow largo movement which follows provides a poetic, reflective return to the conflicts encountered in the first movement. This organization of the music has the effect of heightening the tension. The mood of the third movement is dark and somber, and yet it foreshadows the triumphant climax that follows in the fourth movement. When the section opens, the melancholy beauty of reflective hours is succeeded by the vibrant, active tones of man coming to terms with his fate. The drama is enhanced by strong, resonant rhythms, breaking forth from the tympani in the opening bars, and continuing periodically throughout the movement. The sounds of the tympani and the brass compose a series of triumphant gestures, suggesting man's intense commitment to victory over hostile forces. Shostakovich's symphony provides a remarkable, imaginative vehicle for expressing our emotional life, as it condenses complex meaning within the confines of its relatively limited musical "space." In so doing, it expresses values which go beyond that space.

If we conceive of visual meaning in a way analogous to our discussion of music, it is clear that graphic differences can constitute the real natural base for the artist's visualizations. This is because the graphic differences can be transformed into an interpretive medium, which becomes subject to ongoing development over time. As Margolis observed, cultural structures are like languages in being subject to accidental and deliberate variation in use.[25] Just as the language learner can only master language in use, the cultural practitioner becomes the master of his medium through activities that open the medium to change.

Therefore, when we think of culture as language-like, we think in terms of powers of expression that the individual derives from collective life through personal mastery of the collective forms. As Pierre Bourdieu has described the functioning of cultural regularities, they are "collectively orchestrated without being the product of the orchestrating action of a conductor."[26] This reminds us of Wittgenstein's language games, which are examples of informally coordinated activities displaying regularity without having any single coordinating agent. Since language games can only be mastered in practice, through interaction with other language users, they provide a good model for how we might conceive cultural regularity and cultural change in general.

We can develop this point more fully if we pursue the idea of children at play and think of the ways in which the structures of games function in their play. Gadamer, in *Truth and Method*, offers a provocative comparison between art and play, but in order to carry out the comparison he intends, we must put aside the attitude which regards play as an idle activity. Gadamer insists that play is a process which changes its participants: it is not external to the child, but enters into the formation of his personality. The structures of the game contribute to the child's self-development, since they establish a "to-and-fro movement" which frees the participants to respond to each other in ways not possible outside the game.[27] Gadamer's point is not, of course, limited to the child, since an adult who commits himself to playing a game establishes relationships to other players that alter the meaning of everyone's actions. The "to-and-fro movement" is not limited just to games involving balls and playing fields, because any game has internal dynamics capable of changing the players. Gadamer argues that the participants are required to reenact the game, which provides an impetus for individual actions. "The player experiences the game as a reality that surpasses him."[28]

In parallel fashion, Gadamer sees the work of art as creating an imaginative framework, within which new meanings may develop.

Whether we think of the artist or his public, "the work of art has its true being in the fact that it becomes an experience changing the person experiencing it."[29] Applied to the visual arts, this idea dovetails neatly with Merleau-Ponty's idea about visual frameworks. Just as the players of a game engage in actions which are individual, but regulated, so is the artist's work governed by semantical regulations which he may only partially comprehend. Because of this, Bourdieu characterizes cultural activities as "regulated improvisations."[30] Improvisations on historical practices occur because the inherited cultural patterns do not form closed structures, but almost ask to be changed because they are incomplete. Even when a musical or dramatic text already exists, it is not a closed form. Its enactment in each performance is a temporal act, which requires imaginative re-creation.

It is especially important in this context to reiterate the distinction between generative structures and formal structures. Bourdieu argues from his fieldwork with the Kabyle people in Algeria, for example, that the formal calendar, which is subdivided into discrete days and seasons, is misleading. He even suggests that is is an artificial structure, superimposed by the outside observer, as he seeks to construct a picture of the rhythm of Kabyle life. Contrary to the formal calendar, the native who engages in the rhythm of practical agricultural life employs names for the seasons and for successive periods of the year which do not reflect sharp logical separations. Some of the names for periods of the year have more than one application, and the attempt to construct a completely consistent calendar from native reports turns out to be a baffling activity.[31] Why is this, we may ask. Our temptation is to conclude that the Kabyle are careless about logic, in comparison with the anthropological "scientist" who comes to observe their practices. However, Bourdieu is dissatisfied with such a condescending stance, and argues in contrast that the *practical* calendar has an economy of its own. It makes for fuzziness in the boundaries between periods, but this indefiniteness makes those periods adaptable to changing circumstances each year. The temporal developments of agrarian life require open-ended concepts, which cannot be tied down to the categories of strict logical thinking. He adds: "The fact that symbolic objects and practices can enter without contradiction into successive relationships set up from different points of view means that they are subject to *overdetermination through indetermination*."[32] The practical advantage of having multiple meanings for a term (overdetermination) is that it allows flexible application, and the drawing of attention to activities and situations which are equivalent in practice. This line of thinking is summarized as follows by Bourdieu:

> If ritual practices and representations are objectively endowed with partial, approximate systematicity, this is because they are the product of a small number of generative schemes that are *practically interchangeable*, i.e. capable of producing equivalent results from the point of view of the "logical" demands of practice. If they never have *more* than partial and approximate systematicity, this is because the schemes of which they are the product can be quasi-universally applied only because they function *in their practical state*, i.e. on the hither side of explicit statement and consequently outside of all logical control . . . .[33]

Like Margolis, Bourdieu sees the logic of practice as informal and requiring pragmatic determination. The practical logic entails indetermination because it operates by analogy and strategic response to changing situations in daily life.

If we return now to the consideration of games, we can see why Bourdieu's emphasis on practical logic may be helpful to our study. Since every game involves strategies, games obey a practical rather than strict logic. Strategies can only be developed within the unfolding game. These strategic developments are not merely matters of style, since they effect the substance of the game, just as style effects the substance of art works. However, the player does not encounter strategic alternatives as objective possibilities presented to his consciousness, because the players exist within the activity of the game and can improvise strategies only as called for by the situations of the game. This is what Gadamer means by the "to-and-fro movement" of the game. The movements of the players cannot be determined in advance. If they do not tailor their actions to the emerging patterns of the game, they will not succeed. Gadamer's argument is that art shares this practical logic with games, requiring the artist, or viewer of the art, to approach the work imaginatively, rather than in terms of rigid rule structures. The result may be an enhanced self-understanding, if we give ourselves over freely to the imaginative space created by the work of art.

Bourdieu's whole model for cultural interpretation plays on the idea that culture is governed by the logic of practice. He objects to theories of culture defining it from the spectator's standpoint, because objectivist accounts make it appear that people's actions are simply ritualized forms of behavior, or, alternatively, behavior under a formal code. Neither approach is adequate, and both have insufficient grounding in practical exchanges between people. As Bourdieu puts it: "To substitute *strategy* for the *rule* is to reintroduce time, with its rhythm, its orientation, its irreversibility. Science has a time which is not that of practice."[34] The emphasis on generative structures as temporal structures is important for our understanding of visual culture. It moves us beyond a static idea of regulative structures.

If we think of a game like contract bridge, for example, we can see the force of this remark. Although the partner's bidding is governed by a system of point counts and suit distributions, which control the flow of information in the establishment of a contract, a player cannot afford to treat these structures as if they were rigid standards, or he will be unsuccessful in the game. He must learn how to modify his responses to fit the changing situations of the game or he will miss opportunities for creative strategies which may make the difference between victory and defeat. This observation is also true of the actual playing of the hands, which requires the player to develop a sense of timing so he will know when to finesse an opponent and how to make intelligent guesses about the distribution of the cards. The playing of the game is a temporal enactment of terms set out in advance, but if the player does not approach the application of these terms in a flexible, thoughtful way, he will not fulfill his intention to play well.

In parallel fashion, the artist's intentions reflect the visual practices governing his medium, although they do not begin to approach the formality of the structures governing a game of bridge. Cultural meaning can be discerned by the artist only from within his applied activity, and the creation of a new works depends on the participant learning how to go on from existing visual traditions. Our approach to culture is nonpsychological because the collective orchestration of cultural practices occurs without having to be consciously comprehended. A person may develop his sensibilities without internalizing all of the ways different cultural structures enter into his work. As Bourdieu points out, cultural schemes are "able to pass from practice to practice without going through discourse or consciousness . . . ."[35] Relative invariants in practice may make their presence felt without being discussed or consciously noted, even as invariant perceptual structures of the visible world may function silently in our visual experience. Bourdieu argues that a child may acquire a sense of honor, for example, without much effort, because the rationale for it may be evident from the behavior of adults, without their having to teach it. The sense of honor may reflect, quite simply, the "application of principles coherent in practice."[36] Therefore, human sensibilities may be developed from the informal functioning of meaning structures, without any codification of those structures being necessary.

The view of culture we have developed in this chapter depends on a close relationship between nature and culture. Jakobson's theory of the development of meaning out of sound differences has provided the basis for a generalized account of the emergence of values out of physical differences. In concluding this discussion about cultural regularities, it is important to realize that when sound differences are transformed into musical potentials by making sound into a medium of expression, the *expressive use* of sound is not to be construed as making no difference in the physical reality. On the contrary, although every valuational process has a natural basis, the created meaning requires transformation of natural material from its original form into something else. Therefore, sound differences are altered in being organized into meaningful utterances by human speakers, and into musical phrases by human performers, even as graphic materials (ink marks, pigments, and the like) undergo alteration in being made into paintings and drawings. At the same time, as Gadamer has helped to show, the creator himself is changed in the process, even as the viewer and hearer of works may be if he gives himself over to the created work. The "to-and-fro" movement of cultural practices contributes to the make-up of human nature, because man is as much a creature of culture as he is a creature of nature. Or alternatively, the cultural is natural to man. Geertz's warning about the dangers of stratigraphic interpretation deserves renewed emphasis here. Geertz argues, in fact, that we have no humans apart from cultural reality, since "culture, rather than being added on, so to speak, to a finished or virtually finished animal, was ingredient, and centrally ingredient, in the production of that animal itself."[37] In other words, if we speak of the *human* animal, we must put the emphasis in the right place. One implication of doing so is the recognition that humans appear as naturally disposed to create and study art works as they are to satisfy their biological urges. The one is no less natural than the other.

Even as we recognize the reciprocal working of nature and culture in human life, it is important to distinguish what we have established from the mere recognition of continuity between them. The reason is that evolutionary accounts of culture frequently commit the stratigraphic fallacy by describing cultural reality as a simple extension of natural processes. The theory presented here certainly has treated cultural reality as emergent from nature. Jakobson's account of the emergence of meaning from sound differences points to a strong *dependency* of linguistic meaning on physical differences, but this is a different matter from regarding it as caused by them. The causality of the creative act is an issue we have not directly discussed, and it may appear to some readers that we have destroyed the creative contributions of the mental agent and substituted an unimaginative account of physical causality for it. However, this is not the case.

The issues involved in this area of questioning turn out to be more complex than they might, at first, appear. John Dewey, for example, is very perceptive in his insistence that we distinguish between the infant's spontaneous cries and the *expressive* nature of art works. The former is carried out without knowledge and intention, whereas the artist intentionally employs a medium to express himself.[38] What is confusing here, as Dewey rightly notes, is that both the infant's cry and the artist's expression make use of physical movements. Thus, we need to clarify what the expressive practices of the artist have which distinguishes them from thoughtless, habitual, or spontaneous physical movements. This question has everything to do with how we regard the functioning of cultural regularities because they seem to inform the artist's expressive movements but not the infant's cries. How they do so remains to be discussed in the next chapter.

Meanwhile, let us note that Dewey himself is not always clear about where he stands on the nature-culture question, because his own evolutionary orientation sometimes seems to align him with the stratigraphic approach. Here is what he says about the expressive use of a medium:

The connection between a medium and the act of expression is intrinsic. An act of expression always employs natural material, though it may be natural in the sense of habitual as well as in that of primitive or native. It becomes a medium when it is employed in view of its place and role . . . as tones become music when ordered in a melody. The same tones might be uttered in connection with an attitude of joy, surprise, or sadness, and be natural outlets of particular feelings. They are *expressive* of one of these emotions when other tones are the medium in which one of them occurs.[39]

What this passage leaves unclear is just what interpretation we are to give to phrases like "natural material" and "natural outlets of particular feelings." The latter idea, in particular, is crucial for the understanding of expression in the arts, for if some forms of expression are more "natural" than others, does this leave cultural processes in a subordinate position to those which are "natural?"

What we have shown in this chapter is that the natural differences appearing as phonemic differences can only be identified and used by someone who practices an extant language. That may be Dewey's point in distinguishing the infant's cry from the performer's musical expression of distress, since the infant in unable to identify and use sound differences as a medium of expression, even though he may emit and respond to them. The problem with presenting phrases like "natural outlets" in an evolutionary setting is that it may suggest some precultural condition for man which is more natural than his later, cultural condition.

The force of these remarks can be seen if we remember earlier discussions of Gombrich's cultural schemata, which he describes as variable forms to be judged against standards of "making and matching." If nature is conceived as the model against which cultural forms are to be matched for adequacy, then we have a version of naturalism to which this chapter has been opposed. While Gombrich speaks of the equivalency of forms as alternate representations of reality, we follow Bourdieu in shifting the emphasis to questions of equivalency in *practice*. Geertz's nonstratigraphic approach to the study of man helps to remind us not to make nature the model and cultural forms the derivative inventions whose value is to be judged against the model.

The status of cultural practices as conceived here can be clarified by remembering Merleau-Ponty's insight that "the meaning is not on the phrase like the butter on the bread, like a second layer of 'psychic reality' spread over the sound. . . ."[40] Nor is there a second layer of 'cultural reality' spread over physical reality, since the *use* of sounds in meaningful utterances and in musical expression transforms what they *are*. This raises again the general question of the ontology of art works and the status of the traditions supporting them. That is the subject for Chapter Six.

CHAPTER SIX

Imagination and Cultural Change

O ur inquiry began from Matisse's
The Red Studio (Figure 1), which displays the materials and equipment of
the artist's work space for everyone to see. Matisse self-consciously
reveals the importance of these materials; paint pots, brushes, canvases,
an easel, and other substances which enter into the creation of paintings,
and other materials of the sculptor's art. We may, if we wish, add our
own background of other materials and settings that are transformed
into photographs, video works, musical performances, and the like. In
transforming these materials into art works, the artist must turn them
into media of expression by exploiting physical differences inherent in
them (marks on canvas, sounds, positive and negative space, etc.), and
these differences form the basis of semiotic systems. Although we have
shown how these materials form the grounding for the artist's works, we
have also shown the essential role played by cultural regularities and
values in the creative process. Thus, the works created cannot be
explained solely in terms of their physical make-up because the
surrounding cultural systems obey a logic of their own, not under-
standable in terms of mere physical differences. The language-like
functioning of cultural systems requires us to go beyond the physical
differences that form one basis for their effectiveness.

What else is needed for an adequate explanation of cultural works? Our answer has been framed in terms of the contributions of social conventions in forming systems of meaning. The strategy of this approach has been to insist on the physical grounding of art works without reducing their significance merely to a set of physical characteristics. The dimension of meaning has been introduced by treating cultural regularities as patterns occurring in practices which sustain themselves over time. Thus, we have begun to outline a position on the ontology of art works emphasizing their distinctive cultural dimension without creating a separation of these features from physical reality. This is especially necessary because all art forms make use of physical means of expression.

In developing a diacritical account of language and culture, we have observed that the logic of practice requires informal reasoning within a collective setting, since the meaning of cultural practices can only be determined by contextual judgements drawing from background beliefs and information not directly presented. No one is able consciously to discern all the relevant regularities which structure collective experience—as we have seen from our consideration of games—and so the source of their regulating power must be sought beyond the individual members constituting the collective. In the case of games, the participants engage in a shared activity shaping the behavior of each individual without the whole game having been programmed or planned by any one of the members. This is not to deny, of course, that programs and plans may enter into the unfolding of the game.

These considerations imply that we must put aside accounts of the creative process which attribute sole causal agency to the individual creator. Such accounts are misleading, at best, because they fail to incorporate the contribution made by cultural conventions to the efficacy of the creator's work. While this point does not undermine the primary role played by Matisse in the creation of his paintings, it is quite another matter to interpret his paintings as resulting from his own causal agency alone. We do not have to choose between identifying impersonal cultural forces as causes and attributing the works to Matisse alone, but instead we have shown another basis for understanding the emergence of new art works. The present chapter will develop the account of cultural regularities further, in order to clarify the causal functions entering into the creative process.

We have already established that cultural *regularities* inform the behavior of artists when they create new works, even if those regularities are not consciously intended by the artist. Without this dimension of general meaning, the artist would have nothing to express and his public would have nothing to perceive. This observation does not mean, of course, that art works must have a single, specific meaning that the cultural forms enable the artist to express. On the contrary, we have held that cultural works exhibit an overdetermination of meaning, requiring those who interpret them to exercise practical judgments.

At the close of the last chapter, we began to stress the importance of distinguishing cultural studies from evolutionary approaches modeled on biological functioning. This is a warning that we need to be cautious in our approach to interpreting cultural regularities. Their role in the creative process is easily misconstrued, making it appear that the artist plays a lesser role in creation than he actually does. The cure for too much emphasis on the artist's will is not to displace him from the picture entirely, only to substitute impersonal forces in his place. In further discussing this question, we should recall Geertz's claim that anthropology should be fashioned as an interpretive science oriented toward meaning rather than as "an experimental science in search of law."[1] The model of natural law is tempting, especially in light of contributions evolutionary interpretations have made to our understanding of man. Nevertheless, we should strive to avoid the path of least resistance by treating cultural regularities as forms of objective laws. If we were to do this, we would end up simply transferring the idea of causality from nature to culture without alteration. So viewed, a culture would become a collection of forces surrounding the individual agent and explaining his various actions. However, we have already shown that languages do not operate by having utterances fall under covering laws, but they require interpretive variations on the part of the agent who uses them. This line of reasoning places the concept of cultural *forces* very much in doubt, pointing instead in another direction.

The alternative concerns the idea that "collectively orchestrated" regularities invite individual interpretations and applications, introducing improvisations and changes over time. Although all such regularities depend on physical differences for their logical content, they also depend on an interlocking network of elements that codetermine the significance of the physical differences. Therefore, the diacritical theory of language and culture requires *both* distinctive physical features *and* a generative network of significance. This generative dimension of culture is the collective dimension which no single individual can completely master and comprehend, because it depends for its functioning on the interaction of members of a social group as they mutually determine regularities in applied settings. The general reason for this determination in practice is that changes in one aspect of the generative system produce changes in others as well. We have seen how this codetermination of elements works in relation to color and sound differences in previous chapters.

The ongoing development of music, for example, occurs because existing muscial conventions open up possibilities of novel expression. There can *be* no music without performance and the consequent possibility of variations in practice, not to mention the fact that the valuational context of musical conventions encourages new compositions. Although musical tradition establishes patterns in which the aspiring musician is trained, they are enough like the patterns of linguistic training that they, too, require improvisations as new situations arise. Even the existence of the musical score for the performer does not establish a single way for it to be rendered, since regularities of musical convention do not determine musical valuations in a narrow way. Therefore, the socially-fostered regularities in music leave open new interpretive possibilities, although there may be limits to the innovations that are tolerable within any given tradition (e.g., there may be limits to how much dissonance is tolerable within the system of Western harmonics).

Since the model of objective laws is too strict for explaining cultural phenomena, we need to look elsewhere for an understanding of the creative process. Geertz himself suggests the right approach when he holds that cultural studies need to imitate clinical studies if they are to address the reality of culture adequately. Geertz describes the nature of clinical inference in these terms:

> Rather than beginning with a set of observations and attempting to subsume them under a governing law, such inference begins with a set of (presumptive) signifiers and attempts to place them within an intelligible frame. Measures are matched to theoretical predictions, but symptoms (even when they are measured) are scanned for theoretical peculiarities—that is, they are diagnosed. In the study of

culture the signifiers are not symptoms or clusters of symptoms, but symbolic acts or clusters of symbolic acts, and the aim is not therapy but the analysis of social discourse.[2]

If social discourse is the proper location for cultural studies, then in examining the cultural practices of other people we should make it our ideal "to converse with them."[3] The mutual respect required in genuine conversation implies that the presumptive ingredient in cultural analysis should be the analyst's predisposition to find meaning within the cultural regularities he discerns.

What this means is an approach to cultural systems as significant organizations of actions, governed by rational purposes. Although no one thinks that everyone behaves rationally all the time, the respect due to someone in conversation presumes an element of rationality in what is said, or if not, the diagnosis of what has gone wrong to interfere with the realization of rational purposes. If we approach the cultural analysis of art works in this fashion, what this means is that a work, such as Cezanne's *Bathers*, is to be treated as a token of a type, a concept we can now understand in fairly straightforward terms. For example, the *Bathers* can be treated as a token of Cezanne's own style, since style is a general type with respect to each of the works which exemplify it. For those who are knowledgeable about Western painting, the style of the *Bathers* is transparently Cezanne's. It is an especially good example of his late style, when his handling of brushwork and the construction of bodily images out of color and color gaps had been perfected to a high degree. The judgment of how a particular work exemplifies a style is a "clinical" judgment, similar in this respect to the diagnostic judgments of the psychiatrist as he considers a complex of factors in diagnosing the behavior of one of his clients. Yet we must observe that this judgment, whether in the case of the psychiatrist or the art critic, is not a matter of applying a covering law to an instance. Furthermore, we may apply the type-token distinction to Cezanne's style by treating it as a token of Impressionist or Post-Impressionist works. These cultural traditions, therefore, function as higher-level types in comparison to Cezanne's own style, since his style fits within more general forms of cultural regularity known by these labels. Such a judgment is not, however, a matter of strict causal interpretation.

In an earlier chapter we discussed the way in which Picasso's Cubist paintings appear to emerge from the background of works like

Cezanne's *Bathers*. What is now clear is that we would be stretching a point if we described this relationship to Cezanne's paintings as if they were *causes* of Picasso's Cubism. Nevertheless, they foreshadow Picasso's developments, even as the sense of honor of Kabyle children was said by Bourdieu to have its source in the behavior of their parents. Bourdieu attributed this derivation of honor from the parents to the fact that the children's perception of parental behavior was of something "coherent in practice." What this suggests is that Picasso's derivation of Cubist ideas from Cezanne is, similarly, the result of his perception of coherent visual practices in Cezanne's works.

We can see, therefore, just how far an acknowledgment of cultural sources is from committing us to the view that cultural conventions *cause* the artist to make his works. This conclusion implies another: that to trace anything to *sources* in a clinical diagnosis is not necessarily the same as tracing it to its causes. Or alternatively, one might wish to say, as some interpreters of scientific reasoning have, that the natural sciences are not wedded to a mechanical account of causality.[4] Since that issue takes us too far afield here, let us simply note that an account of scientific explanation might be reconstructed to make the natural sciences a part of the larger hermeneutic approach being outlined here.

That much having been said, we should note that Geertz is emphatic in treating his version of cultural studies as scientific, and he is not willing to concede that the natural sciences are the model for all scientific interpretation. He holds instead that an approach appropriate to the subject matter may still be scientific in a relevant sense, if it involves grounding in empirical oberservations. In this respect his position is close to John Dewey's theory of valuation, since Dewey, too, insists that values can be studied in a scientific way. One aspect of Dewey's program is to avoid basing discussions of value on feelings, because he is wary of mentalistic assumptions that creep into such descriptions. Because of this, Dewey reconstructs his account of valuation in terms of the physical context in which values arise, the behavior manifested in pursuing them, and the social context in which the behavior occurs and in which judgments are made.[5] This makes it possible to approach the study of values contextually, thereby opening up the possibility of scientific correlations of behavior within the social and physical environments.

What this means for the study of art works is indicated by Dewey, when he observes:

Man whittles, carves, sings, dances, gestures, molds, draws and paints. The doing or making is artistic when the perceived result is of such a nature that *its* qualities *as perceived* have controlled the question of production . . . . The artist embodies in himself the attitude of the perceiver while he works.[6]

In framing the interpretation of art in this way Dewey makes it clear that he thinks art is continuous with other forms of cultural practice usually assigned a lower status. If artifacts can be studied scientifically, then art works may be treated as artifacts too. If someone objects that their aesthetic import is thereby omitted. Dewey's reply is that the difference between a carved object having only utilitarian value and one having artistic merit can be formulated in terms of perceptions and how certain perceptual ends controlled the process of production. Perceptions, too, can be studied scientifically.

Rather than our dwelling on the differences of quality between a utilitarian carving and an artistic carving, Dewey's strategy is to conceive the values involved as different ends-in-view that controlled human behavior during their production. He objects to the philosopher's habit of abstracting purposes, or ends, from their context of conception and execution. This he believes, results in distortions in the assessment of value. What such abstraction misses in terms of art is the intimate role played by the medium in the whole creative process. The result is a failure to understand how much the artist savors his medium and how much the means of creation are inherent in the work produced.

Worse than this failure, however, is the fact that some ends which may appear valuable in abstraction may not seem so when coupled with the means to accomplish them. This point is easy to grasp, because we are familiar enough with examples where the means-ends connection has been ignored. If the price of ridding ouselves of troublesome insects, for example, is a form of health-threatening pollution, then the end does not seem so valuable as if we asked only: "Is it desirable to rid ourselves of troublesome insects?" We may answer yes to the latter question and yet decide to forego it when means and ends are considered jointly. Therefore, Dewey urges that we maintain a means-ends continuum in our thinking about values.[7] If we did so, he believes that we would make our conduct subject to more intelligent control. Following such an approach, we would find the scientific study of values having an impact on our lives: "Improved valuation must grow out of existing valuations, subjected to critical methods of investigation that bring them into systematic relations with one another."[8]

The control to be gained in the case of art is through the identification of pertinent relationships that enter into the creative process. This is not, however, a matter of identifying mechanical causes. Among other things, the pertinent relationships include questions of token-type properties, which can only be identified relatively to purposes. Dewey himself recognizes the importance purposes play, and his idea of ends-in-view reflects features of forecasting and planning. That is one reason why he substitutes a means-consequences analysis in the study of valuation for the cause-effect analysis of the natural sciences. Nevertheless, Dewey never implies that causal accounts of physical systems that enter into the creative process are irrelevant. On the contrary, the means-consequences analysis appears as a hierarchical addition to the store of already existing scientific knowledge. This fits with his general emphasis on explanations which maintain the link between the physical and social environments, on the one hand, and those distinctive ends-in-view that are of concern to the artist, on the other.

Dewey believes that the need for exercising intelligent control in the process is very great because the creator must anticipate the perceptual outcomes for those who encounter his work. They, in turn, must enter into an active process of re-creation that parallels features of the artist's own experience in creating the works. The artist has already "selected, simplified, clarified, abridged, and condensed according to his interest,"[9] and Dewey believes that those who would appreciate his work must do so as well. To account for this transaction, Dewey thinks we must attend to the physical, behavorial, and social settings which make it possible.

Dewey's strength is in the focal role he gives to these perceptual elements in the creative process. His position is not far removed from certain features of the one being developed here. Like Dewey, we have highlighted the transformation process by which the artist: (1) coordinates and re-forms physical materials by physical means, and; (2) modifies existing cultural regularities in the process. Dewey emphasizes the importance of the careful consideration of ends-in-view within the creative process, and he holds that the artist's special task is to give unusual emphasis to perceptions. He believes that the utilitarian production of objects would dominate human culture unless the artist had a prior commitment to the values of intense perceptual experience. Dewey argued that no aspect of human activity besides art, with the possible exception of the practice of laborartory research, so well reflects an understanding of the essential role of means-ends coordination. It provides such a good model for value theory because art works exemplify the way a medium inherently contributes to the experiential content it expresses.[10] Cezanne's *Bathers* would not have its distinctive visual content without his intelligently measured use of color, his distinctive brushwork, and the geometric sensibility he cultivated so assiduously.

The attraction of Dewey's approach is that it presents a cohesive picture of the creative process by joining together elements of creative insight, cultural regularity, the centrality of the medium, and the informing of individual actions by common perceptual concerns. At the same time, he presents the cultural changes achieved by a painter like Cezanne as the manifestation of powers of both sensibility and intelligence. We therefore find Dewey's account of the valuational process attractive in many respects.

However, it fails to adequately address Geertz's call for cultural studies based on the realities of social discourse. Although there were many occasions on which Dewey speaks of cultural media as languages,[11] he never develops this theme because of his commitment to a view of culture based on perception. The latter emphasis is natural, given Dewey's evolutionary presuppositions. However, in what follows we will make use of a social discourse view, contrasting Gadamer's ideas of culture with Dewey's evolutionary approach.

The advantage of a social discourse model can only be made clear after examination of several issues, but the first is relatively simple. It concerns the fluidity of developments within conversational exchanges, which exhibit the to-and-fro movement Gadamer attributed to play and extended to his analysis of the functioning of art works. While Dewey's own approach highlights the dynamic nature of cultural systems, given his emphasis on process and context, Gadamer's approach helps to make clear how this fluidity develops from within the nature of the semantical structures themselves. This difference is evident in the following elaboration of the idea of play by Gadamer:

The movement which is play has no goal which brings it to an end; rather it renews itself in constant repetition. The movement backwards and forwards is obviously so central for the definition of a game that it is not important who or what performs this movement. The movement of play as such has, as it were, no substrate. It is the game that is played . . . . The play is the performance of the movement as such.[12]

Two aspects of this passage call for special emphasis: (1) Gadamer's account of cultural systems highlights the way in which cultural regularities or structures provide repeatable forms, and; (2) these forms are conceived as requiring temporal reenactment, which is occasional. The combination of these two features is central to what Gadamer describes as "the transformation into structure,"[13] a phrase he employs to describe the change produced in some material when it becomes endowed with general cultural import. Gadamer believes that the structural aspect of the game creates a reason for its being performed and repeated on many different occasions. Thus, the semantic dimension of cultural systems possesses an autonomy which contributes to its own continuation as a structure, despite temporal change. This feature of cultural systems, coupled with the fact that they have an overdetermination of meaning, accounts for the fact that many different performances that differ in significant ways still count as actualizations of those structures.

While evolutionary structures are also capable of reproduction over time, Gadmer's approach is differentiated from Dewey's by his emphasis on collective activities that enter into the maintenance of cultural structures. The language-like character they possess means no creator or player can control what happens in the collective enterprise, whereas the instrumentalist account Dewey presents calls for the exercise of individual control in an essential way.

This contrast requires further elaboration because it has important implications for the ontology of art. Gadamer holds that the child at play, or the native reenacting a religious ritual, share in common a close identification with the structure of the game or the tribal ritual. Therefore, neither one of them draws a distinction between his self-identity and his identity as player of the game or participant in the ritual. Moreover, such a close identification of humans with cultural structures is, in Gadamer's view, part of the natural make-up of man. "His playing is a natural process. The meaning of his play, precisely because . . . he is a part of nature, is pure self-presentation."[14] The reason for this claim will be clear momentarily, but it involves Gadamer's conviction that cultural regularities express our humanity in a natural way.

This idea contrasts with the notion that the self-identity of humans is grounded on a private consciousness. Gadamer's stance implies that a variety of forms of self-identity enter into a person's life, some of them entailing close identifications such as those just considered. It is worth remembering an argument from Chapter II. We saw there that the modern concept of consciousness is tied to its being the counterpart to objects in nature. In other words, consciousness is *what* takes note of, perceives, thinks about, and intends objects. It is also what directs inquiry and employs methods of investigation. This latter fact different-iates Gadamer's approach from Dewey's. Dewey's instrumentalism retains the aspect of the Cartesian concept of the mind which structures experience by methods.

In contrast, Gadamer's conception of the self-structuring of ac-tivities through games, rituals, or other cultural practices implies that a person gains powers through processes of identification and reen-actment. In other words, the idea of self-presentation through play, ritual, or art concerns the way in which personality develops and the initial way in which a sense of self arises. Identification processes, therefore do not require direction by a center of consciousness, but reflect more subtle developments occurring through participation in the way of life of a culture.

This idea is certainly close to some aspects of Dewey's own concept of development, but in the absence of a clear social discourse model of interpretation, he is not nearly so persuasive as Gadamer in drawing a conceptual picture of that development. The token-type distinction made use of earlier is also pertinent here, because the multiple strands of linguistic overlap characteristic of token-type analysis suggest, as well, the complex features of identification and distinction entering into the formation of a meaningful sense of person. With which type, for example, is Cezanne to identify himself? Is his work to be an example of the genre of bather paintings, of French bather paintings, of French landscapes, of non-Renaissance landscapes, of Cezanne's own later syle, of Post-Impressionist works, or of anticipations of twentieth century abstract art? The answer is, of course, all of these in some measure and in some fashion, the point being that Cezanne, the painter, cannot have a simple identity which predetermines what and how he is to paint.

The implications of this hermeneutic approach are far-reaching, and even the conception of physical nature is shifted by Gadamer's stance. Here is what he says of nature: "Nature, inasmuch as it is without purpose or intention, as it is, without exertion, a constantly self-renewing play, can appear as a model for art."[15] Nature appears here as a self-renewing play of seasons, of growth and decay, of the rise and fall of tides. This concept is a very different affair from the evolutionary interpretation of nature, which, for all its emphasis on changing structures distinctly subordinates change to law-like regularities. This is where Geertz's distinction between forms of cultural analysis modeled on objective law and those modeled on social discourse becomes especially pertinent. The question is what kind of model shapes cultural interpretation. Dewey's own position is somewhat uncertain when he discusses art, and certain features of his comparison of cultural structures to nature come close to Gadamer's conception of the self-renewing play of nature. For example, when Dewey describes the relationship between rhythms in music and painting with rhythms in nature, it sounds strikingly like Gadamer's description above.[16] Nevertheless, Dewey's overall instrumentalist and evolutionary commitments tend more toward nature as a system of objective law.

Gadamer's way of understanding structure as opening itself to occasional variations is also pertinent to an altered conception of truth, a theme which is particularly crucial to the central thesis of this book. Gadamer's idea of the transformation into structure creates a basis for imaginative interpretations that go beyond existing ideas of meaning and truth. Gadamer is paricularly perceptive in his grasp of the interlocking of our idea of truth with the idea of scientific methods, since the conception of truth which treats it as the propositional counterpart to objective structures is precisely what an emphasis on methods of control would be expected to produce. Even when Dewey modifies this tradition in the direction of pragmatic and contextual judgment, he leaves the assumption of an objective background intact. In contrast, Gadamer's idea of open cultural structures eventuates in a notion of truth as disclosure, because the imaginative variation of conceptual structures may eventuate in disclosures of new aspects of reality *through* the altering structures.

How is this possible? Gadamer describes the transformation into structure of games as establishing a *closed* space (the space of the game) within which the movements of the players are, paradoxically, liberated. This is because the closed confines of the game structure release the players from the everyday world of serious purposes. Thus, the transformation into structure may, as Gadamer shows, generate unforeseen alternatives:

> Only through this development does play acquire its ideality, so that it can be intended and understood as play. Only now does it emerge as detached from the representing activity of the players and consist in pure appearance of what they are playing. As such the play—even the unforeseen elements of improvisation—is fundamentally repeatable and hence permanent. It has the character of a work.... In this sense I call it a structure.[17]

This passage contains several features pertinent to the question of truth. What it shows is that by isolating one's formulations in an act of imagination (the parallel here to play), one does not necessarily undermine an intention to seek truth. On the contrary: (1) the structure produced in the imaginative transformation includes elements which are "fundamentally repeatable" (i.e., semantical elements); (2) the repeatable elements may take on different "occasional" manifestations in different formulations; (3) the transformations of imagination result in "pure appearances," as is especially evident in art works, and; (4) these appearances are, nevertheless, capable of disclosing something about reality. Finally, Gadamer's mention of the "representing activity of the players" points to the functional dependence of representations on regularities and variations in structure. This latter point requires further development.

The representing activity of the players, or of an artist or other interpreter, presupposes a certain mode of representation, which helps to determine the content of what they experience. When there is imaginative alteration of the structure itself (a modification encouraged within art), then what is seen or understood undergoes a change in content. In the case of art works, the transforming into pictorial form, for example, is not a simple translation onto canvas of what the artist has seen. It *changes* the content of what is normally seen by creating an imaginative rendering of it. By this means we may gain insight from one of Cezanne's renderings of Mt. St. Victoire because the repeatable visual structures he created have applicability to *our* encounters with mountains, even as it did to his encounter with that particular mountain in Provence. The invention of pictorial forms is not an indifferent matter, but one that equips the artist and his viewers with ideal visual types in terms of which other paintings and other visual experiences can be developed. Accordingly, we see Cezanne as having developed a visual style which, in one sense, was a variation on existing pictorial traditions, but which, in another sense, was the creation of visual *types* that served him, and still serve us, on other occasions of visualization. In this way, his imaginative creation of what Gadamer called "pure appearances" has the effect of producing "an increase in 'pictorialness' to being."[18]

What does Gadamer mean by this idea? He is raising questions about the ontological status of pictures. While we often think of pictures as pale counterparts, lacking the robust reality of the things they depict, Gadamer argues that pictures play a more significant role than this common view suggests. He holds that the intensity of pictorial images created by great artists shows that they *add* something to our experience, by transforming a landscape into something else, or a bowl of fruit into a set of forms that reveals important relationships to our eyes. This intensification of meaning is evident in the Shostakovich symphony, discussed in Chapter V. It does not leave everything as it was before we heard it, because it presents man's struggle in a new and dramatic way, thereby altering our understanding of ourselves. We can also see Gadamer's principle of the transformation into pictorial structure at work, if we examine Leonardo da Vinci's drawing, *A Star of Bethlehem* (Figure 21). This flower is normally seen within its setting in nature, but the richness of its relationships to other things in nature interferes with our examining it with the clarity made possible by Leonardo's drawing. He shows us the elegant unfolding of the flowers from the leaves, and the flowing movements of the leaves in relationship to each other. Leonardo's use of isolation of the flower within the framework of the drawing highlights these features, and creates the "increase in 'pictorialness'" to which Gadamer referred. The types of visual form created by Leonardo were applied repeatedly by him, and later by other artists, in rendering other things visible. Thus, cultural structures establish a semantical context in which there can be a regulated improvisation of visual meaning, and these improvisations are able, in turn, to modify the structures gradually. The artist is especially involved in the growth of visual meaning, the imaginative structures he helps to create transforming the vision of the rest of us beyond everyday perceptions. If Leonardo teaches us to see more perceptively, that is because his work

Fig. 21 Leonardo da Vinci *A Star of Bethlehem*
(C. 1506-1508) Pen & ink over red chalk, 198 × 110 mm. Courtesy of Her
Majesty The Queen, Royal Library, Windsor Castle, England.

opens up possibilities of visual meaning we had not adequately considered beforehand.

When we ask how this is possible, Gadamer's idea of visual semantics provides us with part of the answer. It suggest that we need to reconceive the idea of imagination, to view it as a particular kind of interpretive activity, instead of our thinking of imagination as opposed to reason. The concept of visual regularities may help us to overcome the idea that imagination is divorced from realistic interpretation. Paul Ricoeur, in discussing parallels between painting and language, adds this observation to our thinking:

> Far from yielding less than the original, pictorial activity may be characterized in terms of an "iconic augmentation", where the strategy of painting, for example, is to reconstruct reality on the basis of a limited optic alphabet. This strategy of contraction and miniaturization yields more by handling less. In this way the main effect of painting is . . . to increase the meaning of the universe by capturing it in the network of its abbreviated signs.[19]

The augmentation of meaning Ricoeur refers to is evident in the handling of the flower by Leonardo. His "limited optic alphabet" intensifies our encounter with the reality of the flower.

This is so because structures of cultural meaning carry us from a psychological frame of reference into a broader intentionality framework. Instead of the viewer's experience being confined to a momentary encounter, he acquires a larger interpretive setting which can open up questions and forms of thinking, productive of new insights. The merely transient character of time is thereby transcended, not in the sense that one is made to exist outside of time, but in the sense that the limitations of momentary experience are overcome. Language also helps us to achieve this transcendence of the momentary, by enabling us to classify *this* occasion as an instance of a *type* of thing. In parallel fashion, we have argued that works of art serve the same purpose. An example discussed by Merleau-Ponty reinforces this point. He reports the story of an innkeeper who was confused by Renoir's visit to the sea to study the water in preparation for his *Bathers*, because the painting portrays bathers in an inland setting. Merleau-Ponty argues, in response to this anecdote, that all Renoir needed was "a typical form of manifestations of water."[20] He was exploring the water of the sea to discover invariant aspects of our visual encounter with water. Renoir was seeking a principle by which he could effect the metamorphosis into pictorial structure.

Such principles combine semantical elements with new occasions for their expression. This idea is not, by any means, confined to the sphere of language and the arts, since Gadamer holds that a parallel transformation into structure may be present in religious rituals and festivals. The meaning exemplified in a ritual, for example, goes beyond the priest repeating habitual patterns which make the worshippers comfortable within a religious routine. While any structure has the potential of becoming a deadening form, repeated merely out of habit, the vitality of religion has to do with the potential of the ritual to provoke new insights; what the priest must hope for is that the worshipper will so identify with the movements created by the ritual that spirtual insights will develop from the isolation of the worshipper within religious "space."[21]

Gadamer's point is that the occasional aspect of the transformation into structure has the potential to change even the most well-known rituals or art traditions for those who experience them anew. This line of reasoning helps us to avoid a misconception that might well attend the example of Leonardo's drawing of the flower, since we might easily slip into thinking that the pictorial structure requires only one kind of reading of the image. However, we must ask *what* that structure has contributed. The answer is that Leonardo's use of a certain method of projection (which he, after all, helped to perfect) has the potential of disclosing to us just what a flower *is*, as a self-presenting aspect of nature. In other words, the transformation produced by Leonardo's imaginative depiction is not necessarily confined statically within the limits we may perceive in the method of Renaissance visualization. We may, as active perceivers of Leonardo's work, create an occasion of perception in which Leonardo's visual forms can be activated by our own visual under-standing, educated as it has been by such other artists as Cezanne. The occasion of reenactment does not necessarily have to be confined to the static reception of the original method of projection, so familiar to students of the Renaissance tradition. The self-presenting whole that fascinated Leonardo in the drawing may be rekindled for an imaginative viewer who gives himself over to the working of the structure. Such improvisations are essential to Gadamer's idea of the transformation into structure.

The idea of objective structure returns to haunt us again in this context. We find ourselves tempted to think of Leonardo's contribution as as objective depiction of a real flower, whereas Gadamer insists that we consider the occasion on which reality presents itself to us *through* the visual forms. In like manner, we are likely to think of the temporality of art under presuppositions also deriving from the idea of objective structure. Gadamer, however, challenges us to consider another way of understanding the relationship between occasion and structure, similar to the challenge issued by Bourdieu when he objected to the anthropologist's tendency to substitue a notion of objective temporal order for the practical calendar governing agrarian life among the Kabyle. Both Gadamer and Bourdieu challenge our tendency to treat temporal order as a simple linear structure of succession, which governs our conception of the temporal priority of cause over effect (cause and effect being separate events on the time-line). Bourdieu's comment quoted earlier, that "science has a time which is not that of practice," was allowed to pass without analysis.[22] Now, however, with the help of Gadamer's account of the transformation into structure, we are prepared to clarify what he meant.

To begin with, three observations on the concept of time are in order. First, we have already seen how practical reasoning requires the application of multiple token-type relationships with respect to a given occasion of usage. This occurs because of the overdetermination of meaning that enters into cultural reality. Such overdetermination means that a simple linear causal account inevitably abstracts from germane features of what is being studied. Therefore, Bourdieu was irritated by the failure of fellow anthropologists to admit the overdetermination that enters into the practice of agrarian calendar distinctions. What alternative is there to the idea of objective temporal order, mapped out as a systematic calendar? Bourdieu seems to be suggesting a clinical diagnosis of temporality, where the loose play between different typological patterns has been incorporated into an intelligible account. Thus, he holds that practical time is not identical with strict causal order, nor is it identical with any version of structure which abstracts from the practical necessity of applied judgments about the way a given set of events exemplifies, or fails to exemplify, a seasonal type.

Second, Gadamer's analysis of the structure of games uncovers the functioning of repeatable patterns in practice, which we are able to detect on the different occasions of reenactment of the game. The implied relationship between structure and occasion of reenactment is closer to Bourdieu's conception of variations equivalent in practice than it is to the covering law-instance model.[23] Thus, Bourdieu holds that the anthropologist can find patterns without presupposing objective causal laws.

Third, the linear succession model of time manifests itself as inadequate when we consider certain traditional cultures where ancestors have such an active importance in the life of the people that they are almost contemporary figures. If we think in terms of acts of identification, rather than in terms of actual physical relationships, we may say that these ancestors bear an importance to living individuals that falls outside any objective causal account we might offer.[24] We may, if we wish, dismiss such cultures as "primitive" and claim superiority for our own modes of temporal analysis, but thinkers such as Bourdieu and Geertz exhort us to confront the reality of these modes of interpretation in cultural analysis. In other words, the form of self-identity developed within many native cultures is not assimilable to our model of personal individual consciousness.

These considerations call for a fuller examination of the bearing of temporal order on cultural analysis. In order to deepen our grasp of the language-like nature of cultural systems, we need to consider time in relationship to some linguistic ideas discussed by Jakobson. In discussing Saussure's theory of language,[25] Jakobson observed that Saussure distinguished between two axes of analysis with respect to linguisitic phenomena: the axis of simultaneity, having to do with relationships holding between coexisting linguistic elements, and the axis of succession (our usual notion of linear development). Some interpreters refer to these axes, respectively, as synchronic and diachronic time. Jakobson asks whether the phoneme falls within synchronic time or within diachronic development. This question is puzzling, because Jakobson points to acoustic studies where instruments prove measurable diachronic changes within a given phoneme, which is therefore diachronically complex. But phonemes, in similar fashion, function as coexisting synchronic elements forming the basis for meaningful discourse. Jakobson concludes, contrary to Saussure, that phonemes are both synchronic and diachronic in their make-up, because diachronic change cannot be denied with respect to them, yet they exist as elements within a system of differences that must be present, in some sense, on all occasions of the application of the system.[26]

Nor is this analysis unique to linguistics. A moment's reflection makes it clear that music, for example, exhibits similar features. The development of musical phrases and themes require diachronic development—as musical scores indicate by the successive changes they instruct a performer to follow—but the holistic character of songs, quartets, and symphonies also requires repeated synchronizations from both performer and listener. The musical elements must be synchronized into a single musical "picture," but can only be joined into such a whole through diachronic unfolding. Therefore, the diachronic-synchronic matrix appears as essential to music as it is to language.

Gadamer helps us to generalize this diachronic-synchronic structure by the relationship he draws between structure and occasionality. Although he finds his most obvious examples in areas of performance and ceremony, the idea of the double-axis structure is attributed to all cultural entities. We have already seen that visual practices reflect this same double movement, requiring the interpreter of visual images to actively combine what he sees, even if the image is as familiar as a Leonardo is drawing of a flower. We have made clear, with respect to this example, how important it is to perceive an occasional aspect in the visual reception of the flower image. Indeed, the role of temporality is put in the right general perspective when Jakobson observes that " . . . in a system of values the time factor itself becomes a value. In particular, time with respect to its role in language proves to be a constitutive value of the latter, i.e., to be a linguistic value."[27] This is true of time as a pictorial value as well, as we can see by its contrasting function within Leonardo's drawing and Boccioni's *Muscular Dynamism* (Figure 20).

The ongoing improvisations possible within music and language show that temporal order is more fluid than the concept of objective succession implies. Gadamer's discussion of the transformation into structure accounts for development in an intelligible way, as we can see if we consider a phenomenon like metaphor. According to the diacritical account of meaning, the movement implicit in a metaphor depends on a shift in the type of opposition a term bears to others, creating a new or partially new meaning for the term. Given the existence of a body of meaningful signs in a language, the range of new combinations is practically without limit. If we follow Paul Ricoeur in linking metaphors to the process of predication, we can understand how the change of meaning can occur. As Ricoeur sees it, a metaphor depends for its force on a customary literal meaning, with which it contrasts. If a given term, normally employed as a predicate for a family of words, is transferred to another family, this creates a tension which must be resolved, in order to reestablish a coherent meaning.[28] A simple example may help to clarify his idea: "Her eyes glow." This metaphor transfers the term 'glow' from its natural home in language—where it applies to fires and other things that give off light—to a person's eyes. This change in predication sets up a tension between two uses of 'glow', one literal and the other not. The conflict between these two interpretations is the basis for the creation of new meaning, because the semantical dissonance generated by the metaphor must be resolved.[29] One result of the transfer is that characteristics of fire and light become associated with the woman's eyes. For example, we naturally associate warmth with fires, and so warmth becomes associated with eyes through the metaphor. This opens up an expressive dimension to language, which paves the way for poetic discourse. If we extend this idea to other aspects of culture, we can see that the diacritical theory makes sense of expressive functions in terms of rich associations created within complex meaning structures. In fact, Nelson Goodman has argued that expressive symbols are metaphorical exemplifications of established meanings.[30] This is what he says about the expressive symbol:

> The expressive symbol, with its metaphorical reach . . . uncovers unnoticed affinities and antipathies among symbols of its own kind. From the nature of metaphor derives some of the characteristic capacity of expression for suggestive allusion, elusive suggestion, and intrepid transcendence of basic boundaries.[31]

These characteristics of expressive symbols apply to visual symbols as well as to verbal symbols. We have seen already that Munch's *Madonna* is replete with metaphorical overtones, with the red color creating associations between the warmth of the sun, the harlot's sensual appeal, and the warmth of blood. The history of visual symbols also comes into play in the painting, because red is the color of the inner gown as seen in most Medieval madonna figures. Munch takes full advantage of this symbolism to help establish the visual conflict between sensual harlot and sublime madonna figure. Expressive force is derived from the cultural forms themselves.

The diacritical character of culture, therefore, makes growth of meaning natural, and helps us to understand that informative and expressive functions are convergent. The temptation is to interpret metaphoric usage in merely emotive terms, reserving the literal range of usage for cognitive purposes. However, visual overdetermination is an important part of the *cognitive* content of Munch's painting, and verbal overdetermination in a metaphor adds to its informative value, as well as giving it an emotional dimension. Ricoeur insists upon this point, arguing that: " . . . a metaphor is not an ornament of discourse. It has more than emotive value because it offers new information. A metaphor, in short, tells us something new about reality."[32] Just as we gain information from the environment through a change of perspective, which may expose an occluded surface or alter our relationship to other aspects of the visual layout, so we gain new understanding through the metaphorical expansion of verbal meaning.

Gadamer's social discourse model of culture makes it clear that the principles by which a cultural group interprets reality shapes the members' self-understanding as well. Although this is true, it would be wrong to think that this shaping is by causal force, as if produced by an alien, intruding energy. We have shown, on the contrary, that just as we are concretely intertwined with the things of the visible world, so is our thinking, visualization, perception and emotion intertwined with the cultural practices that sustain us and make possible enriched meaning. These reflections lead to the conclusion that our interpretive activities fall within a general human intention to understand the world. The reasoning of the last two chapters clarifies, however, the way in which the actualization of that intention can only come about through the access provided by cultural regularities. Merleau-Ponty places the right emphasis on this way of thinking when he distingishes human from animal existence in these terms: "Human perception is directed to the world; animal perception is directed to an environment. . . ."[33] By this he means that man seeks coherent interpretations, whereas the animal simply responds to what is immediate. Even with respect to man's most mundane practical activities, we have seen that an implicit coherency may make them spontaneously intelligible.

In a similar vein Ricoeur suggests that "the world is the ensemble of references opened up by every kind of text, descriptive or poetic, that I have read, understood, and loved."[34] If we generalize this idea of the text to include all cultural inscriptions, then visual works become text-like forms that aid us in comprehending the visible world as a coherent totality. While we never experience this totality as such, the abiding assumption of rational functioning is that a coherent background, toward which the regularity of our cultural systems points, exists. Our strong desire for coherent interpretations has to constantly confront the limitations implicit in the fragmented moments of our experience.

The relationship of this view of culture to the traditional idea of the conscious agent should now be clear. The creative process cannot merely reflect the conscious intentions of an individual mind, for it draws from complex, interacting strands of meaning entailed in the transformation into structure. This transformation always introduces a measure of ideality into our experience, permitting imaginative rehearsals of beliefs and actions which, in the arena of daily activity, often are simply done without decision or reflection. But all this means is that the arena of consciousness is one in which we construct a narrative for ourselves from the interpretive materials made available to us through describing, explaining, and questioning what we have encountered. We hardly need add that these activities are public, and reflect communal exchanges which make the private narrative possible. Our strong desire to comprehend what we encounter means that we always *need* a single, contemporaneous presentation of it, but it always appears in fragmentary, occasional ways. This means, Gadamer says, that "contemporaneity is not a mode of givenness in consciousness, but a task for consciousness and an achievement that is required of it."[35]

This hermeneutic view of culture and consciousness contrasts with Dewey's evolutionary naturalism in important respects, the most important of which is Gadamer's rejection of a privileged role for scientific method in the interpretation process. His stance contrasts with Dewey's, who says at the conclusion of his Theory of Valuation:

> . . . the science that is put to distinctively human use is that in which warranted ideas about the nonhuman world are integrated with emotion as human traits. In this integration not only is science itself *a* value . . . but it is the supreme means of the valid determination of all valuations in all aspects of human and social life.[36]

While Gadmer agrees with Dewey in holding that science is a value, or involves a whole range of value commitments, he disagrees with Dewey's assessment that the valid determination of value belongs to the sciences. If art is able to disclose reality, then its role in serving man's truth concerns is just as essential as science's is. Nothing in this line of reasoning requires that we have to choose between art and the sciences for understanding man and how he is related to reality. The contrast between Gadamer and Dewey turns on Dewey's emphasis on methods of intelligent control.[37]

In closing we should note some close parallels between Dewey's concept of the instrumental development of intelligence and Gablik's ideas concerning progress in art. When we considered Gablik's views in Chapter III, we found that she regarded the history of art as exhibiting parallel developments to the child's conceptual development. Accordingly, Gablik treats modern art as the triumph of conceptual maturity, and views modern artists as having attained the ability to present the operational processes of intelligence in visualized form. This advance is made possible by achieving measures of conceptual abstraction not possible at earlier stages of art, which, according to this view, were much more embedded in perceptual reality. Gablik is careful, however, to say that the question of aesthetic value is a separate matter from this question of conceptual advancement.

Gadamer's approach gives us a basis for raising doubts about Gablik's separation of conceptual powers from aesthetic values. His concept of the artist's transformation into pictorial structure features a desire on the artist's part to augment meaning through imaginative development of pictorial possibilities. In other words, the question of pictorial possibilities (a conceptual matter) is not separable from questions about meaning and value. In speaking of the child's delight in games of dressing up and pretending, Gadamer observes that the child's goal is not make-believe, for he "intends that what he represents should exist. . . ."[38] In other words the interlocking relationship between reality and representation is so strong that Gadamer believes a merely aesthetic conception of value is quite beside the point. Therefore, the question of conceptual and aesthetic values is coextensive.

One of the issues on which Gablik and Gadamer also would part company is on the significance of past history for our present understanding. Gadamer believes that the transformation into structure provides semantical autonomy to texts and art works, making it possible for us to identify with Plato, Rembrandt, Shakespeare, Bach, and other great figures from the past. Although they are not of our era, they may *become* our contemporaries through our participating in the active process that their works can occasion. The idea of progress in art has a predictable outcome in the assessment of the value of these earlier stages of cultural development, as is exhibited by the following comment by Gablik:

> For the 'pre-logical', or mystical mentality, the visible and the invisible world form one, everything is fluid, categories are not separate, the individual does not experience himself as separate from the group. The fact that there is no line of demarcation between natural and supernatural worlds, between the material and the spiritual, results in a very different picture of the world from that which our modern scientific world-view gives us.[39]

This striking passage exposes major differences between Gablik's approach to art and culture and the hermeneutic approach being advocated in this chapter.[40] In asserting the priority of the scientific world-view, it undermines the capacity of art to challenge and expose the limits of that world-view; and in treating earlier forms of culture as inferior because of the fluidity of their categories and the absence of sharp distinctions between the individual and the group, it fails to acknowledge the positive benefit to be derived from close social identifications. Presumably these are to be rejected as signs of a primitive mentality. In contrast, the hermeneutic perspective treats previous and native cultures as valuable "texts" which may generate valuable imaginative alternatives worth our consideration.

The creative process manifests collective forms of meaning capable of generating improvisations from perceptive individuals, whose forms of improvisation may, in turn, contribute to the modification of the regularities already governing the collective. Accordingly the artist's imaginative activities have as much to contribute to our understanding as the methodical practices of the scientist, whose experimentations and theoretical intepretations are not an exclusive avenue to truth. Rather than art works explaining and predicting, they open up imaginative possibilities that challenge existing interpretations and help us concretely envision reality anew. We are prepared now to reconsider Heidegger's affirmation of the importance of truth for art.

CHAPTER SEVEN

Creativity and Truth

In Chapter I we examined Heidegger's claim that "art . . . is the becoming and happening of truth." We noted that Heidegger speaks of the *becoming* of truth in works of art, not of their *being true*. This distinction is important, serving to point out Heidegger's historical conception of truth: it concerns the development of meanings within a cultural community and challenges the prevalent tendency to limit truth to correspondence tests. In contrast with the ideal of objective truth, he highlights the power of art works to disclose reality. Since he is thinking of the historical development of disclosures, the possibilities opened up by a work are as important as the established interpretations to which they may appeal. Therefore, the question of the *becoming* of truth goes beyond the issue of the validation of claims, because the imaginative expansion of existing visual meaning may expose limitations not even suspected when we attend only to conflicting claims. The idea that truth in art has more to do with disclosure than with correctness is the central idea of the present chapter. We note that the degree of disclosure is an important factor for us to consider.

Given the analysis of the last five chapters, we are now well prepared to examine Heidegger's idea of truth sympathetically. Before we were ready to do so, we had to clear away misconceptions that blocked our path. The most important of these concerned habits of thought associated with the subject-object distinction. Under the influence of this dichotomy, we are prone to separate the experiencing subject from the world and to treat cultural forms as intervening barriers to our direct grasp of reality. In contrast, we have portrayed the man-world relationship in more intimate terms, reestablishing the artist within the visible world and showing his cultural meanings as the natural formative structures in his experience. Thus, we have argued that man's being in the world is at once physical, linguistic and cultural. Although our experience gives a fragmented exposure to reality, its origins in physical, linguistic, and cultural "space" link us to the world from the beginning, thereby negating any implication that we are separted from the world by a veil of ideas or by cultural blinders. That is why we have insisted on the idea of the creative person, rather than of the creative mind. The result is an account of the artist which acknowledges and emphasizes his contextual dependency, and therefore implies that any truth disclosed in art must be conceived in historical and relativistic terms.

If we are to succeed in demonstrating how creativity and truth are complementary values, the quesion of relativism must be confronted. We usually think of relativism in negative terms, as placing limits on our desire for the pure truth. The relativism of art is clear from our demonstration of the artist's strong dependency on his cultural background. Nevertheless, our interpretation of culture as language-like has been designed, in part, to suggest how this dependence is not a rigid impediment to the artist's freedom. Because we are free to speak new sentences and vocabularies and to invent suggestive metaphors, the dependency of speech and writing on existing linguistic structures does not conflict with the ideal of creativity. On the contrary, we have argued that cultural traditions *enable* us to encounter and portray the world. Therefore, although any tradition has limitations, the open-textured character of cultural systems implicitly invites expansion and supplementation. The natural mistake is to think of specific cultural practices as barriers intervening between us and reality, but it is more appropriate to think of them as giving us access to the world. Unlike colored glasses, which may be regarded as giving a distorted picture of the world, cultural systems are like eyes, which enable us to see in the first place. We cannot see without our eyes. They provide a *specific* mode of access to the world, and while other modes of access are conceivable, that does not make this mode an impediment to clear sight. On the contrary, they provide our only real basis for visual access, supplemented by other forms of access with which they intertwine. The dialectical account of human understanding, which recognizes multiple avenues for overcoming limitations in perspective, undercuts the negative tone of relativistic thinking. Just as our eyes invite us to make further use of their powers, with the result that each act of seeing may enrich our visual understanding, so do cultural meanings yield an enlarged perspective over time.

Therefore, while perspectivism does entail relativism, it does not undermine the importance of truth. Truth remains an ideal for our thought, even when we accept the fact that each of our perspectives is in some measure fragmented. Merleau-Ponty strikes the right note on this issue, when he observes:

> Since we are all hemmed in by history, it is up to us to understand that whatever truth we may have is to be gotten not in spite of but *through our historical inherence*. Superficially considered, our inherence destroys all truth; considered radically, it founds a new idea of truth.[1]

What is this new idea of truth? We will develop an account of it in the remainder of the chapter.

To begin with we will return to a theme from the last chapter: man's desire to attain coherent understanding. We considered ideas of Ricoeur and Gadamer about how semantical structures enter into art. The "transformation into structure" occurs automatically whenever anyone paints, writes, designs, or performs; this means that Gadamer and Ricoeur find an implicit commitment to comprehend the world in all of the arts. Ricoeur treats writing as the prototype for this transformation because it distances an author's presentation from his own psychological situation, exposing what he writes to variations in interpretation. In this respect, every work invites interpretations that go beyond what the creator consciously intended. We also noted Merleau-Ponty's idea that man alone has a world, while animals have only an environment. Ricoeur gives a special twist to this theme:

> Thanks to writing, man and only man has a world and not just a situation . . . . In the same manner that the text frees its meaning from the tutelage of the mental intention, it frees its references from the limits of situational reference. For us, the world is the ensemble of references opened up by the texts.[2]

If we generalize this idea of the text to include paintings, sculptural works, and musical compositons, then we see the force of Ricoeur's observation for our analysis. On this view, the world becomes the correlative of our desire to know: it is that to which our questions are directed and the source to which our thoughts refer. Although we desire complete comprehension of the world, our momentary and limited encounters with reality provide only partial fulfillment of that desire. We never have a master text before us. Therefore, anything encountered in experience occurs against the background of an *implied world*, even though the world as such never presents itself in experience. The shared intention of humans to comprehend this implied totality is one aspect of Heidegger's conviction that art works involve truth. Works of art are oriented toward the world (although not always as directly as in descriptive texts) and so they reflect man's general intention to achieve understanding. This idea does not require, of course, that every artist have this as his conscious purpose. The transformation into structure occurs whenever an artist works within his medium.

Once we have acknowledged the radical finitude of our experience, we may cultivate a more adequate grasp of the world in either of two ways: we may invent methods of study and experimentation designed to expose the general laws governing reality (the way of modern science), or we may opt, instead, for an intensive investigation of the things presented in experience, imaginatively expanding our approaches to them to disclose new possibilities (the way of modern art). As Heidegger sees it, Western artists in following this second approach have disclosed new relationships and dimensions to the world. While scientific and artistic thought have different contributions to offer, both are contrary to skepticism because neither one supports the cry of despair arising from our finitude.

Let us consider the artist's approach through a particular example. Monet spent the final decades of his life painting from his gardens at Giverny. These paintings leave a remarkable record of an artist's intensive exploration of a particular place. The countless paintings Monet produced from this setting include the various versions of the water lilies. If we look at different renderings of this subject, what do we find? We are tempted to see them simply as evidence of the liberation of Monet's style, progressing from the mature Impressionism of the early versions to his late, lyrical abstractions. Monet's painting during this period has often been characterized in just these terms. However, we can equally regard them as evidence of Monet's intensive investigation of the gardens over time, leading him to a more sophisticated grasp which enabled him to disclose new dimensions of their reality. For example, if we consider *Japanese Bridge at Giverny* (Figure 22), Monet presents a full view of one portion of the gardens, rendered in the style of mature Impressionism. There are clearly identifiable objects in the painting: the footbridge spanning the water against the backdrop of trees may be the first thing to catch the eye; the lily pads, floating peacefully on the surface of the water, are surrounded by grasses on the banks, and the gaps between the lily pads reflect the surrounding colors in the water. Monet's mastery of Impressionist means is evident in his subtle handling of color modulations, revealing the nuances of light playing over the familiar things of the garden. When we look at other examples, such as *Waterlilies* in Figure 23, we find Monet's attention directed to a more restricted area of the gardens. Like a close-up shot, his painting zeroes in on water lilies and water alone; anything else which shows through, such as the presence of the surrounding trees and sky, appears through the reflecting surface of the water. Monet confronts us with fine points of relationship between lilies and water, water and sky, and the world implied in the liquid presence of things reflected in water. Again we are presented with subtle transitions of color, made more mysterious because the clearly punctuated spots of red, suggesting the blooming flowers, set up a counterpoint with the indefiniteness of the surrounding watery medium. The rest of the setting is absent from our view, yet implied by the way everything is presented. By isolating our attention on a small section of the garden, Monet has enhanced our grasp of the richness of nature, a richness likely to be lost on the casual visitor to his gardens. When we consider, finally, one of Monet's late, abstract versions of *Water Lilies* (Figure 24, a single panel from a larger work), we find the lily pads hardly discernible at all, and the liquid presence of the gardens dominates. He molds color and form to create the atmosphere of the watery world, and references to familiar things are no longer evident. His isolation of color and light conveys the mood directly and forcefully, yet this painting remains, like the others, an investigation of the gardens. Monet's imaginative interrogation has exposed elemental relationships, and the way he isolates these *elements* in the last paintings increases our sense of the mystery of that place. By detaching our vision from the familiar world of footbridges, tree lines, grass-covered banks, and

Fig. 22 Claude Monet, *Japanese Bridge at Giverny* (1900)
Oil on canvas, 35-⅛″×39-½″. Mr. and Mrs. Lewis L. Coburn Memorial
Collection, Courtesy of The Art Institute of Chicago.

Fig. 23 Claude Monet, *Waterlilies* (1906)
Oil on canvas, 34-¾″×36-¼″. Mr. and Mrs. Martin A. Ryerson, Courtesy of The

Fig. 24 Claude Monet, *Water Lilies* (c. 1920) Oil on canvas, center panel 6'6'' × 14'. Mrs. Simon Guggenheim Fund, Collection, The Museum of Modern Art, New York.

floating lily pads, Monet has disclosed elements of the visible world, which are representative of our larger experience.

Thus, a fragment of the world, exposed for our contemplation, has been freed from the restrictions of our ordinary categories of interpretation. Color and light, which fit into our usual interpretative repertoire, become dominant forces in Monet's rendering of the gardens. Although his vision is *personal*, it takes on general significance. The new idea of truth suggested by this example joins one individual's expression of his intensive relationship to a specific place with the power of his work to disclose elemental relationships to others. This is possible because the dialectical network, to which Monet's work connects, enables him to question and explore the gardens through existing visual conventions, while altering them imaginatively until they are able to convey the richness contained in the gardens. When we think of the water lily paintings in this way, they represent more than changes in Monet's style, displaying more essentially the changes required by his concerted investigations. For this activity the ideal of objective truth seems irrelevant, since questions of validation are less in the forefront than his desire to expose new visual possibilities. Perhaps what Goodman has called "rightness of rendering" is at issue for Monet, but only if we free this idea of any suggestion of validation tests.[3] Since Monet had no neutral rendering with which to compare his own, but had to modify one painting in response to all the others, he was guided by considerations other than validation. Heidegger associates the artist's interest in truth with the desire for authenticity, which can only be realized through the attainment of new visual understanding.

The intensive relationship established by art works contrasts with the distancing act of objective thought. Although the act of framing does, in some sense, distance the presented image, it nevertheless can intensify our relationship to aspects of the visible world. Like the religious ritual, Heidegger sees the great work of art establishing an intensive focus, which opens up its subject matter to thoughtful development. If we recall that works are things in the world, they may, like anything else, undergo changes of significance and stimulate altered interpretations over time. The outcome of these developments is largely unpredictable. Although completed works seem to be finished objects, Heidegger finds this appearance misleading, because he thinks their meaning goes on being created by those who preserve and view them.

Therefore the question of objective correlation is beside the point for this conception of truth in art. The power of art is more subtle and indirect than any descriptions. Heidegger points to the Greek temple as an instance of the indirect power works have to provoke temporal development:

> A building, a Greek temple, portrays nothing. It simply stands there in the middle of the rock cleft valley. The building encloses the figure of the god, and in this concealment lets it stand out into the holy precinct through the open portico. By means of the temple, the god is present in the temple . . . . It is the temple work that first fits together and at the same time gathers around itself the unity of those paths and relations in which birth and death, disaster and blessing, victory and disgrace, endurance and decline acquire the shape of destiny for human being. The all-governing expanse of this open relational context is the world of this historical people.[4]

The temple served literally as a gathering place for the people, as they made periodic sacrifices to the gods. It also served them, and still serves us, as a visual and conceptual "gathering place," capable of revealing sea, sky, and the rhythms of life within the frame of its majestic columns. While the temple helps us to comprehend the mentality of an ancient people, its power extends to the formation of our own. The setting sun, seen through the mysterious monuments of Stonehenge, or the sky framed by a Greek temple, takes on an ambience which alters our understanding of what they are and what they have to offer. In the broadest terms Heidegger sees this same potential in all great art. Just as the temple is more than a building, paintings are more than just pictures, because they form an "open relational context" tending toward ongoing cultural development. If we recur to our idea of the condensed image, we can appreciate the force of this Heideggerian line of thought. The metaphor of the "gathering place" suggests how art fosters dialectical development by teasing our visual imagination into action. Man the thinker, man the questioner, encounters in art a basis for the ongoing development of his understanding.

A particularly fascinating implication of Heidegger's approach to art is his idea that works of art both reveal and conceal. Just as the temple opens out to the surrounding landscape, while hiding its contents within, so works of art set forth a vision, while concealing what is behind or outside the frame. This is necessary because of the grounded, physical nature of both temple and painting. In Heidegger's categories, they are both of the *earth*. He speaks of art as something which takes place between world and earth; the opening up or setting forth occurs within the limitations of the earthy materials, which are opaque rather than transparent. This is one way in which Heidegger insists that we come to terms with the limited, temporal character of our interpretations. Full acceptance of their historical character entails recognition of the double movement of interpretation between revealing and concealing. These limitations apply to language as well as to any other cultural form. Yet it would be misleading to say that we know no truth because our interpretations are earthbound. What we understand is actually understood, whatever its limits may be.

Nevertheless, we are still tempted to skeptical conclusions. Why is that? The temptation to join Nietzsche in the hyperbole "There is no truth," threatens to overcome us just when we embrace Ricoeur's definition of the world as the "ensemble of references opened up by every kind of text." Put quite simply, there is no single master text. Because we have also argued that no aspect of experience is foundational for all other aspects, we appear to be confronted with nothing more than an array of conflicting texts. However, the situation is not so bleak as it may seem. What we must remember is that cultural interpretations are linked to practice. Before any problem of competing interpretations surfaces, we find ourselves in contact with the world through a body of reliable beliefs. Although doubts may be raised about any particular belief or perspective, we nevertheless cannot put them all in question at once. Because of this, Richard Rorty, in arguing against generalized forms of skepticism, has held that:

> . . . "the world" will just be the stars, the people, the tables, and the grass—just those things which nobody except the occasional "scientific realist" philosophers think might not exist. The fact that the vast majority of our beliefs must be true will, on this view, guarantee the existence of the vast majority of the things we now think we are talking about.[5]

If we begin from the context of established beliefs, which have already proven themselves to some extent in practice, then our questioning arises from a desire for more adequate beliefs, rather than from any need for a wholesale change of view. While this relativism of beliefs makes impossible a simple application of the true-false alternative, that does not mean our interest in truth thereby becomes compromised. If we now apply this idea to the visual arts, what we discover is that an artist like Monet begins from what has already been *successfully* visualized, and then turns to the challenge of extending his grasp of the visible world. The expressive power gained by an artist when he revises familiar ways of seeing is not, in this sense, opposed to a desire to depict the things of the world. The investigation of visual reality can never begin from a blank slate, nor can it recur to foundational visual experiences as testing points for a proposed perspective.

Therefore, although the variety of cultural and individual vantage points tempts us toward conventionalism or toward skepticism, when we look at a work like Leonardo's *Star of Bethlehem* (Figure 21), we cannot doubt the availability of reality to the probing eye and the skilled hand. Thus, the dialectical conception of truth, shared by thinkers like Heidegger, Merleau-Ponty, Ricoeur and Gadamer, stresses the artist's power to supplement existing temporal perspectives through questioning and exchange. Gadamer's analogy between art and play helps us to see that each act of picturing the world is a temporal enactment, which depends for its significance on a context of meaning, inevitably carrying us beyond the momentary point of origin. Monet's personal vision, extends beyond the limits of the gardens and beyond his own period in history.

The ambience created by Monet's water lilies also has the potential to substantially alter how we see the world. Thus, its subject matter is secondary to this larger articulation of visual meaning, although he probably could not effectively achieve it without grounding it in a specific theme. The whole semantical substructure of painting, therefore, makes it more than the expressive gesture of an individual subject, and more than the representation of particular places and things. When Monet's painting entered a more abstract phase, he may have gained, in fact, in his ability to make explicit the semantical forces available in all of art. In addressing the question of how we are to understand the contributions of modern painting, with its increasing emphasis upon abstraction, Merleau-Ponty has argued that:

> Modern painting presents a problem completely different from that of the return to the individual: the problem of knowing how one can

communicate without the help of a pre-established Nature which all men's senses open upon, the problem of knowing how we are grafted to the universal by that which is most our own.[6]

Merleau-Ponty underscores the twentieth century loss of confidence in a simple, preestablished structure of nature, which can be uncovered apart from the relativity of interpretations. He sees modern painters as having comprehended and emphasized this relativity. At the same time, he insists with Heidegger that, rather than this pointing to a "return to the individual," it points toward the "problem of knowing how we are grafted to the universal by that which is most our own." What do we make of this paradoxical assertion?

It is paradoxical because, on the face of it, the variety of cultures and languages appears to point away from anything universal. Nevertheless, Merleau-Ponty insists that cultural creations of different ages have meaning for other people, pointing toward "the unity of culture" and the artist as a participant in "a single art."[7] This paradoxical claim deserves careful attention. In a particularly puzzling passage, Merleau-Ponty comments on this paradox by observing:

> But this is a problem only if we have begun by placing ourselves in the geographical or physical world, and by placing works of art there as so many separate events whose resemblance or mere connection then become improbable and calls for an explanatory principle. We propose on the contrary to consider the order of culture or meaning an original order of *advent*, which should not be derived from that of mere events, if they exist, or treated as simply the effect of extraordinary conjunctions. If it is characteristic of the human gesture to signify beyond its simple existence in fact, to inaugurate meaning, it follows that every gesture is *comparable* to every other.[8]

They are comparable because the nature of cultural reality is replete with diacritical crosscurrents, and the momentary gesture is not *confined*, in the same way that a body in space is confined to a particular location, or an event to the mere moment. With regard to culture, Merleau-Ponty is arguing agaist the notion that a particular work, or a particular gestural act, has only a local bearing. Thus, his idea that cultural acts belong to an order of *advent*, having the potential to be catalysts for other works and gestures, is specifically designed to oppose an objective account of culture. The self-generative character of cultural systems keeps them from ever being merely local in their import. Even though specific works originate in local circumstances, they reverberate with overtones of concerns common to other historical agents.

In this context it is especially important to notice that Merleau-Ponty rejects, as well, any notion that cultural reality is reducible to physical reality, even though he is a strong advocate of the essential role played by embodiment. We find, in fact, what we would expect from earlier chapters: Merleau-Ponty denies that cultural causality is "second causality" and adds that "cultural creation is ineffectual if it does not find a vehicle in external circumstances."[9] This emphasis on the embodiment of the creator, and his dependency on a physical medium for expressing himself, does not imply, however, that cultural entities can be adequately treated as like so many bodies in space. The themes of embodiment and advent are joined into a provocative synthesis by Merleau-Ponty, who insists upon both: (1) the personal and local character of art works, and; (2) their general significance, which derives from the implicit universality of man's cognitive concerns.

To get a clearer idea of just how these two factors are consistent with each other, we need to attend to a distinction drawn by Merleau-Ponty between two kinds of history—a distinction he makes while discussing the history of painting. He holds that the museum gives us one kind of history, which he characterizes as the history of forgetfulness, in which we impose our perspective on the past. The resultant conception of history is purely diachronic, reconstructing an account of the past in terms of periods and styles which lead to their outcome in the present. The other kind of history is "constituted step by step by the *interest* which bears us toward that which is not us and by that life which the past, in a continous exchange, brings to us and finds in us . . . ."[10] In other words, this second view of history highlights the potential for exchange that occurs, if we will permit it, when we encounter an alien perspective. The potential for dialogue with the past is what has led, in Merleau-Ponty's view, to the creation of new paintings. Here we find history giving birth to its own development. While the museum gives us a chronological account of paintings, arrayed on a time line, to help give manageable form to our grasp of them, the actual working history requires the painter to gather together strands from the past which enliven his work, and to which he can give a new direction. He does so in terms of his interest, but *this* understanding of his interest links his own interests to those of previous painters. He discovers *his* interest in the working tradition of painting, which calls for him to go on to create more paintings.

If we think of cultural history simply as a chronological organization of events, we fall prey to historicism, which transfers the idea of causality from nature to history. However, the fact that "every gesture is *comparable* to every other" in the order of meaning makes historical derivation different from linear causal derivation, and makes anthropological and historical analyses akin to clinical inference. We will only find this idea puzzling if we persist in thinking of history in a way which separates individuals and eras, and which ignores the synchronic dimension of history. If we were to shift to a conception of history centered around the development of meaning, rather than one centered around the causality of events, we would arrive back at Heidegger's idea of the dialectical development of art.

One of the advantages of the conception of culture as language-like can now be clarified. If we think of the individual language user and the historical background from which he draws his speech acts, we encounter a distinct challenge to a theory of history which explains what happens purely in terms of individual actions and individual events. In considering such issues in *Twilight of the Idols*, Nietzsche argues:

> For the individual, the 'single man', as people and philosophers have hitherto understood him, is an error: he does not constitute a separate entity, an atom, a 'link in the chain', something merely inherited from the past—he constitutes the entire *single* line 'man' up to and including himself.[11]

In an individual's speech acts, we can see evidence of how he draws from a whole background, which (with allowance for exaggeration) may be said to "constitute the entire *single* line" leading up to that act. The whole of English, for example, seems to be required for the writing of this sentence. Human history enters equally into the expressions of the individual visual creator, even though the *way* it enters may not even be evident to him. This is the reason why Heidegger holds that "creation is a drawing, as of water from a spring."

This drawing from the past occurs without the necessity of a conscious effort. We spontaneously evoke those features of the past with which we have already identified ourselves; or, in the case of language and painting, with those modes of expression from the past which we have mastered, and which have therefore become a part of our expressive repertoire. The distance we often associate with the past is put in doubt by this line of thinking, because it reverses the way we think of the structure of time and asks us to recognize how identification of ourselves with a tradition gives substance to what we may become. If we recognize this identification, which occurs naturally in our historical being, then we will endorse an additional point which Gadamer notes:

> Time is no longer primarily a gulf to be bridged, because it separates, but it is actually the supportive ground of process in which the present is rooted. Hence temporal distance is not something that must be overcome . . . . In fact the important thing is to recognize the distance in time as a positive and productive possibility of understanding. It is not a yawning abyss, but is filled with the continuity of custom and tradition, in light of which all that is handed down presents itself to us.[12]

For Nietzsche, and for Gadamer too, the question of the development of *mankind* stands behind my own capacities to think, to speak, and to express myself. This is what Merleau-Ponty has in mind when he holds that the whole history of painting is *one* history. Any visualizations achieved by past artists are potentially meaningful for us, if we make the effort to understand them.

Gadamer especially insists on the absence of captivity in the face of relativism. He points out, for example, that our native language, which appears to set stringent limits on us in comparison to the variety of languages we might speak, actually enables us to master a foreign language. We move *from* linguistic competencies already acquired *to* new linguistic achievements. He concludes that any "language in which we live is infinite in this sense, and it is completey mistaken to infer that reason is fragmented because there are various languages. Just the opposite is the case."[13] Even if we quibble with his claim about infinity, the force of Gadamer's observation remains. Our historical mastery of language, which is temporally and culturally specific, is filled with opportunities for expansion and development beyond these specific conditions.[14] And so is all of culture.

The working of the imagination is the key to this whole line of thought, and it is clear from what we have been saying that imagination and reason are not opposed aspects of our psyches. On the contrary, the idea of truth we have been pursuing requires that we think of the world as available to us through the fluid development of our interpretations. The very idea that we can test out ideas or pictures by a direct comparison with reality has been completely undermined by our analysis. Imaginative development of interpretations becomes an essential feature of the new idea of truth we have been outlining.

The contrast between this new idea and traditional notions of objective truth is made clear in a penetrating analysis by Wittgenstein of our desire to achieve final and compelling interpretations. What we desire, he says, is "an unambiguous picture-language, a language consisting of pictures painted in perspective."[15] This would, according to the theory being questioned by Wittgenstein, provide us with an interpretation on which inquiry could come to rest. However, this is an impossible account of the process of interpretation, as Wittgenstein goes on to show:

> "Only the intended picture reaches up to reality like a yardstick. Looked at from the outside, there it is, lifeless and isolated." — It is as if at first we looked at a picture so as to enter into it, and the objects surrounded us like real ones; and then we stepped back, and were now outside it; we saw the frame, and the picture was a painted surface. In this way, when we intend, we are surrounded by our intention's *pictures*, and we are inside them. But when we step outside intention, they are mere patches on a canvas, without life and of no interest to us .... Let us imagine we are sitting in a darkened cinema and entering into the film. Now the lights are turned on, though the film continues on the screen. But suddenly we are outside it and see it as movements of light and dark patches on the screen.[16]

If we are in no position to find a direct yardstick for our interpretations, where does that leave us? At Wittgenstein sees it, living within our perspectives puts us alternately into and out of "pictures," with their variations depending on the intentionality that governs the activity. Thus, with shifts of our interest the status of the things presented is likewise changed, similar to the way our attention may alter from being inside a film to observing it as so many movements of light on a screen. If this line of thought is accepted, the radical character of the new idea of truth requires that we give to imagination a central role in our quest for truth, because it is through imagination that we can achieve this "inside-outside" shift.

This imaginative shifting of intentional perspectives is something artists are practiced at carrying out. That is why Nietzsche looked to artists as typifying an attitude he saw as exemplary, in contrast to the attitude he attributes to moralists and philosophers of the past. What is essential to that exemplary attitude? For Nietzsche it is the celebration of things as they appear, without any vestige of the idea that they hide ultimate reality from our eyes. It is the idea, attributed to Cezanne by Merleau-Ponty, that the artist is committed to "the exact study of appearances."[17] Cezanne, he believed, subordinated the dream of a completed, stable account of the world to the *process* of studying it as it presents itself. Nietzsche is harsh in criticizing the tradition of Western philosophy for featuring the distinction between appearance and reality, and is especially critical of Kant for his idea that truth concerns things in themselves. Nietzsche makes his case in these terms:

> To divide the world into a 'real' and an 'apparent' world, whether in the manner of Christianity or in the manner of Kant . . . is only a suggestion of decadence—a symptom of *declining* life . . . .That the artist places a higher value on appearance than on reality constitutes no objection to this proposition. For 'appearance' here signifies reality *once more*, only selected, strengthened, corrected . . . .[18]

Nietzsche identifies two errors associated with this distinction. The first concerns the failure to see that the appearances, as they are created and explored by artists, present reality *once more*. Hence, Nietzsche sees the artist as accepting the historical limits of experience and engaging in the "exact study of appearances." Monet in his gardens, and Cezanne meditating before his various landscapes, embody the prototype Nietzsche seeks in a higher form of man, who can get along without the support of any ultimate perspective. Another error concerns Nietzsche's idea that, in addition to appearance-reality serving as a cognitive distinction, it serves also as an evaluative one. It denigrates the world as it appears, and expresses a desire for something better. This evaluative preference of the moralist, who desires a more perfect world than the one he finds, is not shared by the artist, who savors the appearances and alters our vision of them by exposing their beauty and complexity.

Nietzsche's objection is that moralists like Kant simply cannot abide the world *as it is*.

In contrast, he believes that artists practice the highest form of realism and truthfulness. We will have more to say about this theme in the final chapter, where we will consider some ramifications of our study of art for ethics. For the present, Nietzsche's way of understanding the artist is just the approach we need to connect creativity with truth. Because the artist savors the richness of the world, therefore finding it necessary to return to it again and again, the creative imagination plays an essential role in the artist's interest in truth. Hans Hofmann, in speaking of the artist's response to the world, puts the emphasis in this way: "The creative process lies not in imitating, but in paralleling nature—translating the impulse received from nature into the medium of expression, thus vitalizing this medium."[19] The vitalized medium gains in its capacity to disclose what is there, and contributes to the emotional and cognitive development of the artist. In this sense, the question of truth is involved in the development of self-understanding by the artist, and the development of ours whenever we encounter his works.

The argument of Merleau-Ponty that modern art presents us with the question of how we are "grafted to the universal" is linked to this very point. He does not accept the idea of a reality behind or beneath the one presented in our experience, and his reference to the universal is the reference to the particular commitment of man, the questioning thinker. Heidegger's disclosure model of truth treats culture from the vantage point of this commitment, and is governed by the belief that we all share an intention to understand the world. Even the relativity of our perspectives, which looks so threatening when we encounter alien cultures, produces the occasion for dialogue rather than despair. Merleau-Ponty's new idea of truth, which gives an exposition to Heidegger's idea, directs us to the context of dialogue. Here is how he says it:

> This provides a second way to the universal: no longer the overarching universal of a strictly objective method, but a sort of lateral universality which we acquire through ethnological experience and its incessant testing of the self through other persons and the other person through the self.[20]

This testing of the self is the central idea in the claim that "art . . . is the becoming and happening of truth." The visions created by artists play an essential role in our quest for self-understanding, and the imaginative development of their rational powers, perfected by them to such a high degree, gives us a model to follow in our own search for understanding.

CHAPTER EIGHT

Art and Self-Understanding

The new idea of truth considered in Chapter VII is really a variation on a very old idea, derived from Socratic thought. The Socratic version of dialectical thinking began from the established beliefs of his Greek contemporaries, which he subjected to sustained critical questioning. What guided this process of questioning? For Socrates it was the desire for self-understanding, governed by two considerations: the need to resolve perplexities associated with existing traditions, and the conviction that no human interpretation can be final. The problem of conflicting interpretations was the keynote of his thought, and his search for practical wisdom was directed by the desire to achieve more reasonable interpretations. In similar fashion, twentieth century dialectical thinking begins from conflicts in belief, but the array of viewpoints is even more perplexing, raising fundamental doubts for us about what is true and how we ought to live. Modern artists have been especially sensitive to the variety of existing perspectives and have experimented freely to create additional interpretive possibilities. Nevertheless the dialectical search for reasonable interpretations, and its commitment to the idea of truth, remains relevant to these modern concerns.

When we recall Wittgenstein's example of a viewer in the cinema whose attention shifts from "inside" the action of the film to the "outside" perspective of flickering lights on the screen, an especially troubling aspect of the problem of interpretation confronts us. The human capacity to move from the inside to the outside of a given perspective raises serious questions about when we can strike the right posture for enhancing our understanding. Perhaps no artist has been more aware of this problem than Picasso, whose *Girl before a Mirror* (Figure 25) symbolizes the outcome of our analysis. When we ponder this painting, we find no clear dividing line between what shows within the mirror's frame and what shows outside it. Picasso here reveals the multiple vantage points which contribute to our visual grasp of the woman over time. Simultaneously, he poses the problem she must also face when confronted by the mirror: whatever self-image she has already formed comes up against the reality of the mirror, which may enhance, distort, or undermine her understanding of who she is. This uncertainty about the mirror image attaches also to our change of vantage point between pictures and physical reality, social situations and their physical settings, and the different cultural frameworks. The flexibility gained by these inside-outside movements enables us to assume a variety of masks, creating a problem of self-understanding that goes deep, even as it enlarges our freedom.

Picasso's own development reflects a deepening understanding of this problem of different masks, running from his Blue Period paintings of various tragic scenes through his encounter with African masks, his many Cubist experiments, and later works such as *Girl before a Mirror*. These changing interpretations of the human situation are symptomatic of twentieth century man's loss of confidence in a stable ontological background, and consequent uncertainty about who he is and what he should do. The role of art in contributing to our self-understanding, given this lack of secure ontological grounding, forms the subject of this final chapter. We will include in these considerations the question of what art has to contribute to our ethical understanding.

While ethics may at first appear remote from the concerns of modern artists, whose emphasis on the immediacy of color and form has made it seem that expressive power is a specialized concern, separate from any other interest, Picasso's theme of the masks shows that this is not so. If we think of ethics in Socratic terms—as the practical outcome

Fig. 25 Pablo Picasso, *Girl before a Mirror* (1932, March 14) Oil on canvas, 64″×51-¼″. Gift of Mrs. Simon Guggenheim, Collection, The Museum of Modern Art, New York.

of the search for self-understanding—then modern art's ability to expose emotional nuances and to increase the artist's depth exploration of a personal vision has ethical significance. The key to this line of thought is provided by Gadamer, when he addresses the significance of the immediacy of art:

> . . . of all the things that confront us in nature and history, it is the work of art that speaks to us most directly. It possesses a mysterious intimacy that grips our entire being, as if there were no distance at all and every encounter with it were an encounter with ourselves.[1]

The capacity of a painting like *Girl before a Mirror* to create an "encounter with ourselves" gives Picasso the ability to raise disturbing questions. His ironic presentation of the human interpreter's situation indirectly expresses the new ethical situation for twentieth century man.

What exactly does this painting reveal? When we consider the visual ambiguities posed by Picasso, we must come to terms with the absence of any single interpretive framework by which they might be resolved. The radical finitude of our perspectives is clearly suggested by Picasso, symbolized by the way the mirror emerges from within the decorative space, appearing almost like a window opening up from within. Such a theme is common to many twentieth century artists, whose keen sense of varied interpretive standpoints shows up again and again. The way the mirror is placed in Picasso's painting reminds us of Matisse's continuing experiments with windows, picture frames, and doorways, appearing in his paintings both as breaks within a fluid visual field and as natural extensions from within. Matisse's own concern with inside-outside movement is clear when we think of how these rectangular openings, like the goldfish bowls in some of his other paintings, serve as focal lenses for their surroundings, although without any hint of an objective vantage point.[2] Thus, both *Girl before a Mirror* and many of Matisse's paintings confront us with our immersion in a world of appearances, where the assumption of a given, stable background must be put aside. Unlike Alberti's window, which was supposed to open unproblematically into the world, Picasso's painting emphasizes how uncertain we are of our bearings, even though it provides clues for a reasonable context of interpretation.

These considerations suggest that modern artists may have accepted Nietzsche's idea that art focuses on the appearances, with no reference being made to a prior reality. We recall that Nietzsche perceived an evaluative aspect in the appearance-reality dichotomy, instead of treating it as a merely cognitive distinction. This turns out to be important for our consideration of the ethical import of art. Here is what Nietzsche says:

> "The *real* and the *apparent* world"—I have traced this antithesis back to *value* relations. We have projected the conditions of *our* preservation as predicates of being in general. Because we have to be stable in our beliefs if we are to prosper, we have made the "real" world a world not of change and becoming, but one of being.[3]

The concept of the real world tempts us to dismiss interpretation conflicts as signs of our own ignorance, whereas they are more indicative of the situational limits of human experience. The belief that these limits can be transcended by scientific methods tempts us to think we can overcome these limits in other ways as well.

For example, Nietzsche points out that a thinker like Kant treated moral thinking as directed toward a realm outside its grounding in customs. Kant sought the stability of moral law, in contrast with Nietzsche's artist, who celebrates the variety of appearances. Nietzsche insists that the Kantian attitude denies the human terms in which value can be realized. In contrast, he thought that the immediacy of art gives it the power to confront us with a world of change and becoming. When we acknowledge the historical nature of art works, we see that both the world they reveal and the works themselves participate in becoming and change. For art, therefore, we need not introduce an assumption of abiding value, whereas the traditional conception of morality does seem to require that assumption. We can respond to this contrast in either of two ways: for Nietzsche the response is to see in art the possibility for a new moral attitude, whereas others may respond by seeing only opposition between art and morality. This latter response, which modern artists have contributed to by presenting themselves as a band of moral anarchists, arises from a particular understanding of the moral point of view. Nietzsche's alternative, on the other hand, requires a more Socratic approach. Nietzsche saw in the artist's acceptance of a world of appearances the birth of an attitude which promised an end to reliance on the moral law. Gadamer addresses such a theme, when he extends his idea of the immediate power of art in this way:

In comparison with all other linguistic and nonlinguistic tradition, the work of art is the absolute present for each particular present, and at the same time holds its word in readiness for every future. The intimacy with which the work of art touches us is at the same time, in enigmatic fashion, a shattering and a demolition of the familiar. It is not only the "This art thou!" disclosed in a joyous and frightening shock; it also says to us: "Thou must alter thy life!"[4]

The power of art to undermine the familiar, together with its capacity to intensify our encounter with the world, opens up possibilities for change of self. That is precisely why Gadamer compared art to play, since he regarded the openness of play as creating a change in the participants. This idea is the key to Nietzsche's notion that the artist exemplifies desirable ethical traits.

In contrast with the openness of the artist, Nietzsche portrays the traditional moralist as looking for security, following the safe path wherever possible. The assumption of ontological stability is essential to this moralist's stance. In fact, Kant linked his own quest for the moral law to the objective, methodical inquiry of the scientist, his idea of moral law being the logical equivalent of the scientist's natural law. Thus, his idea that ethical reasoning, controlled by a desire for a single imperative binding on *all* rational agents, contrasts sharply with Nietzsche's idea of the artist's free, imaginative play with appearances, and with the delight he saw artists taking in the value possibilities they contain. Gadamer's theme that art can produce a "shattering and demolition of the familiar" adds to the contrast with Kant's ethics, pointing toward a more critical approach to values favored by Nietzsche.

Nietzsche holds that the moralist's valuational approach is one response to our need for a simplified account of the world. The ideal of 'the real world' permits us to project our purposes with confidence. Nietzsche regards that as a sign of the intention "to deceive oneself in a useful way; the means, the invention of formulas and signs by means of which one could reduce the confusing multiplicity to a purposeful and manageable scheme."[5] His understanding of "logicizing, rationalizing, systematizing as expedients of life"[6] is not a negative assessment of rational powers. On the contrary, these belong to a family of activities (simplifying, organizing, formulating, unifying) which enter into all creative work and enable the artist to transform the confusing array of appearances into intelligible form. It is just that no single, underlying unity has to be postulated to make these activities possible, and there is no need to negate appearances in favor of a perfect "spiritual" world.

This Nietzschean conception of the artist fits well with the dialectical conception of reason we have outlined, and his artist expresses an openness to possibilities of dialogue with alien perspectives. We can see this, for example, in Picasso, whose Cubist breakthrough resulted, in part, from his own fascination with the African mask. Picasso's perception was that African art put *himself* to the test, because his modern Western conception of the world was undermined by his taking the African sculptural figures seriously. Instead of dismissing them as signs of a primitive mentality, he took them as mysterious challenges to modern assumptions which accord no place to fetishes and voodoo objects. In fact, Picasso complained that Braque, who was also captivated by African art, failed to accept it on its own terms, seeing it only as a technical challenge to Western art. Picasso, in contrast, discovered a mysterious power in these works to uncover forces of nature long ignored by scientific man.[7]

This example recalls Merleau-Ponty's idea, discussed in the last chapter, that the encounter with other cultures is part of a continuing test of the self. Picasso's response to the test was to create a new form of art, *integrating* the African with the Western. This exhibits the attitude Nietzsche approved in the artist, and which he did not find in the moralist. The stability of moral law seems to be most easily attained where a traditional culture is isolated and where behavioral expectations can be mapped out neatly, reflecting a world view which represents them as demands imposed by the gods. Clifford Geertz has observed that, where there is a close coordination between world view and ethos, "morality has . . . an air of simple realism, of practical wisdom." Violations of morality are therefore signs of irrationaltiy and the unworthiness of the violator for membership in the community. Geertz adds that: "In Java . . . small children, simpletons, boors, the insane, and the flagrantly immoral are all said to be 'not yet Javanese,' and, not yet Javanese, not yet human."[8] Such an attitude is diametrically opposed to the creation of the new man, called for by Nietzsche.

The ethical challenge implicit in modern art is, therefore, associated with its openness to a variety of perspectives, reflecting our loss of confidence that any given perspective is supported by the gods and that any one reflects a natural moral law. The new idea of truth implies a new idea of ethics. What exactly is this idea? The clue to it is contained in the power of art works to overcome familiar ways of interpreting the world, suggesting as it does the need to cultivate flexible responses to situations encountered in life. If we think of the ethical substance of our lives in terms of face-to-face relationships, the immediacy of these relationships challenges us to create them so that, like art works, their value is contained within themselves. An aesthetic morality requires us to assess each encounter anew, without fixed obligations to define our responses in advance. Nietzsche sees the artist as a person willing to take the given materials of the earth and transform them until they reveal something of value.

In parallel fashion, the given relationships we have with other people, and institutional patterns already in existence, form the only material basis we have for ethical value. We must create value out of the relationships we experience, rather than finding it in independently defined patterns of behavior. If we think of two people who desire to establish an intimate relationship, then we can see the necessity for the creation of value on this direct basis, for the quality of their lives will depend on their willingness to accept the actual personalities of each other, modifying their responses to attune themselves to the other. The actual basis of the relationship, like the materials of the earth for the artist, sets limits to what they can accomplish. Just as the artist concentrates on the "transformation into structure" of the given materials, so too people must transform themselves, until they establish a new structural unity. Thus, an ethics built on the model of the creative artist—with its teaching, "Thou must alter thy life!"—is an ethics responsive to the becoming of experience, and what it immediately demands.

The challenge to create ethical bonds is particularly pertinent for modern man, because the cultural complexity we face makes easy coordination of ethos and world view unlikely. Like Picasso's woman looking in the mirror, we must deal with uncertainty concerning what is real and who we are, and therefore we cannot fall back on the "simple realism" of behavior Geertz attributes to traditional cultures. While this tempts us to revert to an individualistic model for ethics, with its implied moral anarchism, the aesthetic morality advocated here is geared toward the creation of shared meaning, even where a single world view is lacking. Thus, *we* need to create our morality, not *I* must create one alone. In approaching this task, the Socratic idea of reasonable interpretation replaces the ideal of a single, uniquely authoritative account.

Nietzsche held, in fact, that "it is only as an *aesthetic phenomenon* that existence and the world are eternally *justified*."[9] This statement shifts our orientation from validation tests, in which we fit particular behaviors to general moral laws, toward a new justification strategy emphasizing the productivity of relationships and the value they contain within themselves. How are we to judge this? The question itself tends to suggest the wrong kind of answer, orienting us toward preexisting standards rather than forcing us to create standards, as we must do in response to changing styles and works in art. This is just what Picasso forced his contemporaries to do when he synthesized features of African and Western art and created a new form of art. The value of his new works could only be judged from the works themselves, and subsequently new standards were derived from them that reflected their appeal. Nietzsche believes that higher forms of action and relationship will, in similar fashion, speak for themselves and point toward different standards.

The critical question to ask here concerns the quality of life created by the actions we take. Here simple realism has to yield to something akin to the fluidity of play, since the overdetermination of meaning attaching to art works also reappears in the field of human actions. We have seen that our gestures do not confine their meaning to simple boundaries, any more than the condensed images of painting do. Gadamer adds an important consideration when discussing the power texts and art works have to move us:

> When we understand a text, what is meaningful in it charms us just as the beautiful charms us. It has asserted itself and charmed us before we can come to ourselves and be in a position to test the claim to meaning that it makes. What we encounter in the experience of the beautiful and in understanding the meaning of tradition has effectively something about it of the truth of play. In understanding we are drawn into an event of truth and arrive, as it were, too late, if we want to know what we ought to believe.[10]

Gadamer's emphasis on understanding as an *event* has its parallel for our thinking about ethics. Just as he thinks that the work of art so draws us to itself that we cannot easily gain a perspective *outside* it, which would enable us to judge "what we ought to believe," so an ethical commitment to create fruitful relationships establishes an intention requiring us to avoid judging in advance what we ought to do. Although an inside-outside perspective shift is possible *after* the fact, it remains true that, while we are creating our actions we exist within the space of the intentions governing them. This intentionality framework is a complicating factor, no less than the overdetermination of meaning which attaches to actions, and an imaginative response is required of us, rather than one which simply replicates patterns of law-like behavior. Thus, we are called upon to operate more like the artist than the scientist in our ethical life.

While these observations only form the beginning of an analysis of how art may contribute to ethics, enough has been said to set the direction of Nietzsche's thought for our present purposes. It is especially important that we avoid thinking of creativity as the act of an isolated, individual subject when applying this aesthetic ideal to morality. That is one reason we have insisted on conceiving the creative act as a cultural development, akin to language, and Nietzsche's own thinking leads to a similar conclusion, as reflected in the following striking passage found in his notes:

> The aesthetic state possesses a superabundance of means of communication, together with an extreme receptivity for stimuli and signs. It constitutes the high point of communication and transmission between living creatures—it is the source of languages. This is where languages originate: the language of tone as well as the languages of gestures and glances. . . .
>
> Every mature art has a host of conventions as its basis—in so far as it is a language. Convention is the condition of great art, *not* an obstacle.
>
> Every enhancement of life enhances man's power of communication, as well as his power of understanding . . . .[11]

This eloquent statement links the central concerns of this book together. Rather than the expressive powers of the artist being portrayed as gestures originating from an isolated subjective source, we have interpreted them as exemplifications of meanings arising from the artist's historical background.

The community that the work of art founds may, nevertheless, not yet fully exist. That is an additional reason why Nietzsche looks to the artist as a model for how we might live, since the artist's imaginative approach to living contributes change to history. While he surely must draw from tradition in creating his works, the integration of this tradition into a new form of art changes its meaning, giving it a new impetus and founding new relationships. As Merleau-Ponty has also argued:

> The painter and the politician moulds others much more often than he follows them. The public he aims at is not given; it is precisely the one which his works will elicit. The others he thinks of are not empirical "others", defined by what they expect of him at the moment. He thinks even less of *humanity* conceived of as a species which possesses "human dignity" or "the honor of being a man" . . . . No. His concern is with others [who] become such that he is able to live with them.[12]

The artist's works will help to create the community promised by his own imaginative outlook. This understanding of history makes it clear how modern man may respond to the variety of interpretations he encounters. Rather than despairing at the loss of a stable ontological grounding, we may regard it as an opportunity for creating our history anew. These considerations lead to an additional note from Merleau-Ponty:

> The history that the writer participates in . . . is not a power before which he must bend his knee. It is the perpetual conversation carried on between all spoken words and all valid actions, each in turn contesting and confirming the other, and each recreating all the others.[13]

The question of which words and actions are valid remains to be determined, judged by their power to disclose reality and future possibilities for community.

In our desire for a simplified view of life, this philosophical perspective may not appear very satisfying, yet it addresses the actual conditions of life. While we might like the life of reason to eventuate in simple formulas and rules of procedure, we must actually evolve it from conflicting currents, requiring from us a sustained, imaginative development of our thinking. This dialectical account of reason makes clear the open-ended nature of thought, made necessary by our shifting emotional involvements and the emerging complications in our experience.

The ideal of the rational mind, with which it contrasts, was fashioned by Descartes to stress the discipline of scientific methods. The failure of the idea of the rational mind to measure up to these demands stems, in part, from its separation from the life of imagination.

This last observation returns us to the contrast from which we began our analysis: the contrast between laboratory and studio. What has the studio to contribute to our understanding, and how does it supplement what we learn by scientific methods? If we think again of Matisse's *The Red Studio*, the absent artist's return will bring into play the imaginative intelligence of a thinker, grounded in a tradition and with skills sharply honed. Surrounded by his own past works, he is free to explore them for new interpretive possibilities that await his definition. The studio is a free place, where man's rational, emotional, and sensual powers have reached a high stage of development, and it represents the kind of atmosphere which encourages further examination of who we are. If the artist is to succeed in contributing to our understanding of self and world, he must first arrive at a refined grasp of his own powers, and how they can disclose new truth to him. Essential to this task is the artist's own style, which we have shown to be far more important than a mere means of expression. Style, for the artist, constitutes the form of his being in the world. That is why Nietzsche criticized Wagner so severely for what he saw as Wagner's superficial music. He charged that Wagner "simply did not require the higher lawfulness, *style*. What is elementary is sufficient— sound, movement, color, in brief the sensuousness of music."[14] Nietzsche saw this failing as critical, because he regarded an artist's style as the fruition of a way of thinking, and a way of approaching life, which gives the power to his work. The studio provides the possibility of creating higher modes of expression, starting from the given reality of what has already been accomplished.

The Nietzschean concept of sublimation is central to his idea of aesthetic rationality. The studio is the place where the sensuousness of man's nature, and the limitation of his modes of understanding, undergoes transformation into higher forms. These new visions, which open the way to fuller disclosure of reality, are what makes truth relevant in art. Sublimation in this sense overcomes the old opposition between feeling and reason and requires that the artist commit himself to the painful process of *self-overcoming*, which is the chief component in his creative act. Seen in this light, when we trace the works to be created back to the absent artist of Matisse's studio, we trace it back to the only source it could have. Yet what this requires is the self-overcoming of the limits of the artist's own past. The development of his style, like the thought of the Socratic thinker, remains essential to the creative process. Merleau-Ponty summarizes the outcome of our study in these words:

> The painter does not put his immediate self—the very nuance of feeling—into his painting. He puts his *style* there, and he has to master it as much in his own attempts as in the painting of others or in the world.[15]

That is what the work of the studio entails. Rather than the creative mind, it requires the sustained development by a creative person of eye, hand and cultural perspective. This idea of aesthetic rationality challenges our inherited ideas about the life of the mind because it makes clear the integral demand for bringing all our powers of emotion and imagination to bear in expanding our understanding. That is why artists go on picturing the world.

Bibliography

Altieri, Charles. *Act and Quality*. Amherst: University of Massachusetts Press, 1981.

Arnheim, Rudolph. *The Genesis of a Painting; Picasso's Guernica*. Berkeley: University of California Press, 1962.

Arnheim, Rudolph. *The Power of the Center*. Berkeley: University of California Press, 1982.

Arnheim, Ruldolph. *Visual Thinking*. Berkeley: University of California Press, 1971.

Barr, Jr., Alfred H. *Matisse, His Art and His Public*. New York: Museum of Modern Art, 1951.

Barr, Jr., Alfred H. *Picasso: Fifty Years of His Art*. New York: The Museum of Modern Art, 1946.

Barzun, Jacques. "The Meaning of Meaning in Music: Berlioz Once More." *The Musical Quarterly*, Vol LXVI (January 1980).

Bernstein, Leonard. *The Unanswered Question*. Cambridge: Harvard University Press, 1976.

Bernstein, Richard J. *Beyond Objectivism and Relativism*. Philadelphia: University of Pennsylvania Press, 1983.

Bourdieu, Pierre. *Outline of a Theory of Practice*. Trans. Richard Nice. Cambridge: Cambridge University Press, 1977.

Brody, J. J. *Mimbres Painted Pottery*. Albuquerque: University of New Mexico Press, 1977.

Dewey, John. *Art as Experience*. New York: Minton, Balch and Co., 1934.

Dewey, John. *Experience and Nature*. Chicago: Open Court, 1926.

Dewey, John. *The Quest for Certainty: A Study of the Relation of Knowledge and Action.* New York: Minton, Balch and Co., 1934.

Dewey, John. *Theory of Valuation. International Encyclopedia of Unified Science*, Vol. 2, No. 4. Chicago: University of Chicago Press, 1939.

Eggum, Arne. "The Theme of Death." In *Edvard Munch: Symbols & Images.* Washington: National Gallery of Art, 1978.

Flam, Jack D. *Matisse on Art.* New York: Dutton, 1978.

Gablik, Suzi. *Progress in Art.* New York: Rizzoli Publications, 1977.

Gadamer, Hans-Georg. *Philosophical Hermeneutics.* Trans. and ed. David E. Linge. Berkeley: Univ. of California Press, 1976.

Gadamer, Hans-Georg. *Truth and Method.* 2nd ed. New York: The Seabury Press, 1975.

Geertz, Clifford. *The Interpretation of Cultures.* New York: Basic Books, 1973.

Gibson, James J. *The Ecological Approach to Visual Perception.* Boston: Houghton Mifflin Co., 1979.

Gombrich, E. H. *Art and Illusion.* 2nd ed. Princeton, N.J.: Princeton University Press, 1961.

Gombrich, E. H. *Meditations on a Hobby Horse.* 3rd ed. New York: Phaidon Press, 1978.

Goodman, Nelson. *The Languages of Art: An Approach to the Theory of Symbols.* New York: The Bobbs-Merrill Co., 1968.

Goodman, Nelson. *Ways of Worldmaking.* Indianapolis: Hackett, 1978.

Gottlieb, Carla. *Beyond Modern Art.* New York: Dutton, 1976.

Hanson, Norwood Russell. *Patterns of Discovery.* Cambridge: Cambridge University Press, 1965.

Heidegger, Martin. *Nietzsche: The Will to Power as Art.* Trans. David Farrell Krell. New York: Harper & Row, 1979.

Heidegger, Martin. *Poetry, Language, Thought.* Trans. and ed. Albert Hofstadter. New York: Harper & Row, 1971.

Hess, Hans. *How Pictures Mean.* New York: Pantheon Books, 1974.

Hofmann, Hans. *Search for the Real.* Ed. Sara T. Weeks and Bartlett H. Hayes. Cambridge: M.I.T. Press, 1967.

Iser, Wolfgang: *The Act of Reading.* Baltimore: John Hopkins, 1978.

Jakobson, Roman. *Six Lectures on Sound and Meaning.* Trans. John Mepham. Cambridge: M.I.T. Press, 1981.

Jaynes, Julian. *The Origin of Consciousness in the Breakdown of the Bicameral Mind.* Boston: Houghton Mifflin Co., 1977.

Kandinsky, Vassily. *Concerning the Spiritual in Art.* Trans. M.T.H. Sadler. New York: Dover, 1977.

Krauss, Rosalind E. *Passages in Modern Sculpture.* New York: Viking Press, 1977.

Langer, Suzanne K. *Feeling and Form.* New York: Scribner's, 1953.

Langer, Suzanne K. *Problems of Art.* New York: Scribner's, 1957.

Lee, Sherman E. *Chinese Lanscape Painting.* Rev. ed. New York: Harper and Row, n.d.

Linker, Kate. "Meditations on a Goldfish Bowl: Autonomy and Analogy in Matisse." *Artforum*, Vol. 19 (1980).

Malraux, Andre. *Picasso's Mask*. Trans. June Guicharnaud with Jacques Guicharnaud. New York: Holt, Rinehart, and Winston, 1976.

Margolis, Joseph. *Art and Philosophy*. Atlantic Highlands, N.J.: Humanities Press, 1980.

Margolis, Joseph. *Culture and Cultural Entities*. Boston: D. Reidel, 1984.

Merleau-Ponty, Maurice. *The Primacy of Perception*. Ed. James M. Edie. Evanston: Northwestern University, 1964.

Merleau-Ponty, Maurice. *Sense and Non-Sense*. Trans. Hubert L. Dreyfus and Patricia Allen Dreyfus. Evanston, Ill.: Northwestern University, 1964.

Merleau-Ponty, Maurice. *Signs*. Trans. Richard C. McCleary. Evanston: Northwestern University, 1964.

Merleau-Ponty, Maurice. *The Visible and the Invisible*. Ed. Claude Lefort, trans. Alphonso Lingis. Evanston, Ill.: Northwestern University, 1968.

Nietzsche, Friedrich. *Beyond Good and Evil*. Trans. Walter Kaufmann. New York: Random House, 1966.

Nietzsche, Friedrich. *The Birth of Tragedy*. Trans. Walter Kaufmann. New York: Random House, 1967.

Nietzsche, Friedrich. *The Case of Wagner*. Trans. Walter Kaufmann. New York: Random House, 1967.

Nietzsche, Friedrich. *The Will to Power*. Trans. Walter Kaufmann. New York: Random House, 1968.

Nietzsche, Friedrich. *Twilight of the Idols*. Trans. R.J. Hollingdale. New York: Penguin, 1968.

Panofsky, Erwin. *Meaning in the Visual Arts*. Garden City, N.Y.: Doubleday, 1955.

Panofsky, Erwin. *Renaissance and Renascences in Western Art*. Stockholm: Almquist and Wiksell, 1968.

Ricoeur, Paul. *Freud and Philosophy*. New Haven, Conn.: Yale University Press, 1970.

Ricoeur, Paul. *Interpretation Theory*. Fort Worth, Texas: Texas Christian University Press, 1976.

Rorty, Richard. *Philosophy and the Mirror of Nature*. Princeton, N.J.: Princeton University Press, 1979.

Rorty, Richard. "The World Well Lost." *The Journal of Philosophy*, 69 (1972). Reprinted in Richard Rorty, *Consequences of Pragmatism*. Minneapolis: University of Minnesota Press, 1982.

Russell, John. *The World of Matisse*. New York: Time-Life Series, 1969.

Saussure, Ferdinand de. *Course in General Linguistics*. Eds. Charles Bally, Albert Sechehaye, and Albert Riedlinger, trans. Wade Baskin. New York: Philosophical Library, 1959.

Sellars, Wilfrid. "Empiricism and the Philosophy of Mind." In *Science, Perception and Reality*. New York: Routledge and Kegan Paul, 1963.

Sontag, Susan. *Styles of Radical Will*. New York: Farrar, Straus and Giroux, 1969.

Spinoza, Benedict. *Ethics*. Trans. W.H. White, *Spinoza Selections*, ed. John Wild, New York: Scribner, 1930.

Stevens, Wallace. "The Man with the Blue Guitar." In *The Collected Poems*. New York: Knopf, 1955.

Taylor, John F.A. *Design and Expression in the Visual Arts*. New York: Dover, 1964.

Whitehead, Alfred North. *Science and the Modern World*. New York: The Free Press, 1925.

Wittgenstein, Ludwig. *Philosophical Investigations*. 3rd. ed., trans. G.E.M. Anscombe. New York: Macmillian, 1958.

Wittgenstein, Ludwig. *Zettel*. Ed. G.E.M. Anscombe and G.H. von Wright; trans. G.E.M. Anscombe. Berkeley: University of California Press, 1967.

Notes

CHAPTER ONE   REPRESENTATION AND TRUTH

1   Martin Heidegger, "The Origin of the Work of Art," *Poetry, Language, Thought*, trans. and ed. Albert Hofstadter. (New York: Harper and Row, 1971), p. 71.

2   Heidegger recalls the Greek conception of truth as *aletheia*, which he associates with "unconcealedness." On this point see *Poetry, Language, Thought*, p. 36.

3   An artist such as Jasper Johns shows us the painting *process* in the finished works. His paintings of number series are a case in point, since he shows us stages through which the painter must move in order to give us a complex image as result. The brushwork, too, is allowed to show and yet is cleverly masked at the same time. Many modern artists exhibit this same explicit self-consciousness, but so do traditional painters, like Rembrandt, whose knowledge of brushwork, layers of paint, and other factors suggests the same self-awareness.

4   The idea that a work of art condenses a complex content in one image is found in Erwin Panofsky, *Meaning in the Visual Arts* (Garden City, N.Y.: Doubleday, 1955), p. 14. This same principle is found in Suzanne Langer, *Feeling and Form*, (New York: Scribners's, 1953) p. 243.

5   For detailed description of this process see Rudolph Arnheim's excellent study *The Genesis of a Painting: Picasso's Guernica*, (Berkeley: University of California, 1962).

6   Maurice Merleau-Ponty, "Cezanne's Doubt," *Sense and Non-Sense*, trans. Hubert L. Dreyfus and Patricia Allen Dreyfus. (Evanston, Ill.: Northwestern University, 1964), p. 19.

7   Maurice Merleau-Ponty, "Eye and Mind," *The Primacy of Perception*, ed. James M. Edie and trans. Carleton Dallery. (Evanston, Ill: Northwestern University, 1964), p. 164.

8   Nietzsche's ideas on simplification appear in several places. See especially *Beyond Good and Evil*, trans. Walter Kaufmann. (New York: Random House, 1966), paragraph 24 and *The Will to Power*, ed. Walter Kaufmann. (New York: Random House, 1968, paragraphs, 516–522.

9   Friedrich Nietzsche, *The Will to Power*, paragraph 616. My emphasis.

10   We should note here that the image we often have of children's play is misleading. Fantasy is not as unrelated to reality as we sometimes think. Gadamer has argued that "children's delight in dressing-up . . . does not seek to be a hiding of themselves, a pretence, in order to be discovered and recognized behind it but, on the contrary, a representation of such a kind that only what is represented exists. The child . . . intends that what he represents should exist." Hans-Georg Gadamer, *Truth and Method*, 2nd ed. (New York: The Seabury Press, 1975), p. 102.

11   Alfred North Whitehead, *Science and the Modern World* (New York: The Free Press, 1925), p. 51.

12   Nietzsche, *The Will to Power*, paragraph 616.

13   Merleau-Ponty, "Cezanne's Doubt," *Sense and Non-Sense*, p. 19.

CHAPTER TWO   EXPRESSION AND FEELING

1   Vassily Kandinsky, *Concerning the Spiritual in Art*, trans. M. T. H. Sadler. (New York: Dover, 1977), p. 19.

2   The distinction between the representative and the representational, although appearing in many sources in aesthetics, is discussed by Charles Altieri, *Act and Quality*, (Amherst: University of Massachusetts, 1981), pp. 289–290.

3   Suzanne K. Langer, *Problems of Art*, (New York: Scribner's, 1957), p. 59.

4   Ibid, p. 91.

5   Suzanne K. Langer, *Feeling and Form*, (New York: Scribner's, 1953), p. 241. My italics.

6   Langer, *Problems of Art*, pp. 29ff.

7   Friedrich Nietzsche, *The Birth of Tragedy*, trans. Walter Kaufmann, (New York: Random House, 1967), p. 34.

8   Friedrich Nietzsche, *Twilight of the Idols*, trans. R. J. Hollingdale. (New York: Penguin, 1968). See the section titled "The Four Great Errors," pp. 47–54.

9   Nietzsche, *Birth of Tragedy*, p. 49.

10   Arne Eggum, "The Theme of Death," *Edvard Munch: Symbols & Images*, (Washington: National Gallery of Art, 1978), p. 153.

11   Quoted by Eggum, in *Edvard Munch: Symbols & Images*, p. 146.

12   Hans Hess, *How Pictures Mean*, (New York: Pantheon Books, 1974), p. 56.

13   Langer, *Problems of Art*, p. 72.

14   Ibid., p. 80. Italicized in original.

15   Jack D. Flam, *Matisse on Art*, (New York: Dutton, 1978), p. 48.

16   Goodman discusses exemplification in two of his books. See his *The Languages of Art*: (New York: The Bobbs-Merrill Co., 1968), Chapter II; and *Ways of Worldmaking*, (Indianapolis: Hackett, 1978), pp. 11-12 and 63ff.

17   Goodman, *Ways of Worldmaking*, pp. 63-64.

18   Maurice Merleau-Ponty, *Signs*, trans. Richard C. McCleary, (Evanston, Ill: Northwestern University, 1964), p. 52.

19   Paul Ricoeur, *Freud and Philosophy*. (New Haven, Conn.: Yale, 1970), p. 46.

20   Ludwig Wittgenstein, *Zettel*, ed. G. E. M. Anscombe and G.H. von Wright; trans. G. E. M. Anscombe. (Berkeley: University of California, 1967), paragraph 486.

21   Ibid., paragraph 492.

22   Ibid., paragraphs 489-490.

23   Rosalind E. Krauss, *Passages in Modern Sculpture*, (New York: Viking, 1977), p. 26.

24   Krauss' interpretation of Rodin's sculpture is close to the whole view we have been developing in this chapter. See especially *Passages in Modern Sculpture*, Chapter I ("Narrative Time"), pp. 27-28. She says of Rodin's figures "They are about a lack of premeditation, a lack of foreknowledge, that leaves one intellectually and emotionally dependent on the gestures and movements of figures as they externalize themselves. Narratively, in relation to the doors, one is immersed in a sense of an event as it coalesces, without the distance from that event that a history of its causes would bestow. With the *Gates* as a whole . . . one is stopped at the surface." Ibid., p. 28.

25   Wittgenstein, *Zettel*, paragraph 487.

26   Merleau-Ponty, *Signs*, p. 75.

CHAPTER THREE   VISION AND LANGUAGE

1   Heidegger, *Poetry, Language, Thought*, p. 76.

2   E. H. Gombrich, *Art and Illusion*, 2nd ed. (Princeton, N.J.: Princeton University, 1961), p. 385.

3   Susan Sontag, "The Aesthetics of Silence," *Styles of Radical Will*, (New York: Farrar, Straus and Giroux, 1969), pp. 12-15.

4   Langer, *Problems of Art*, p. 61.
5   Leonard Bernstein, *The Unanswered Question*, (Cambridge: Harvard University Press, 1976), pp. 39-41.
6   Wolfgang Iser, *The Act of Reading*, (Baltimore: Johns Hopkins, 1978), p. 129.
7   See Rudolph Arnheim, *The Power of the Center*, (Berkeley: University of California Press, 1982).
8   Gombrich, *Art and Illusion*, p. 88.
9   Ludwig Wittgenstein, *Philosophical Investigations*, 3rd ed. trans. G. E. M. Anscombe. (New York: Macmillan, 1958) , p. 194.
10   On this point see Alfred Barr, Jr., *Picasso: Fifty Years of His Art*, (New York: The Museum of Modern Art, 1946), pp. 54 and 57.
11   Gombrich, citing Wofflin, makes the point that "all pictures owe more to other pictures than they do to nature." E. H. Gombrich, *Meditations on a Hobby Horse*, 3rd ed. (New York: Phaidon Press, 1978), p. 9. The importance of pictorial traditions is evident in the studies painters do of earlier masters' works. For an especially revealing account of such influences see the excellent work by Andre Malraux, *Picasso's Mask*, trans. June Guicharnaud with Jacques Guicharnaud. (New York: Holt, Rinehart, and Winston, 1976).
12   Nietzsche, *The Birth of Tragedy*, p. 65.
13   Wallace Stevens, "The Man with the Blue Guitar," *The Collected Poems*, (New York: Knopf, 1955), p. 165.
14   Gombrich, *Art and Illusion*, p. 87.
15   Ibid., p. 39.
16   Ibid., p. 85. See also pp. 292-295 for further discussion of these ideas.
17   Langer, *Problems of Art*, p. 66.
18   Wittgenstein, *Philosophical Investigations*, paragraph 19.
19   Suzi Gablik, *Progress in Art*, (New York: Rizzoli Publications, 1977). See especially a chart summarizing these stages, p. 43.
20   Ibid., p. 85.
21   Ibid., p. 15. Also pp. 9 and 29.
22   Merleau-Ponty, *Signs*, p. 77.
23   For further discussion of these principles see Erwin Panofsky, *Renaissance and Renascences in Western Art*, (Stockholm: Almquist and Wiksells, 1968), pp. 120-129.
24   The full title of this painting is *The Third of May, 1808: The Execution of the Defenders of Madrid*. Alternatively it is known as *Third of May, 1808, at Madrid: The Shootings on Principe Pio Mountain*. This is a companion piece to Goya's *Second of May, 1808*.
25   I am indebted to Dan Davidson, a painter at Alfred University, for some of these observations about Mimbres pottery. For a published analysis of Mimbres pottery see J. J. Brody, *Mimbres Painted Pottery*, (Albuquerque: University of New Mexico, 1977).

26   For an analysis of Chinese landscape painting, an excellent source is
      Sherman E. Lee, *Chinese Landscape Painting*, rev. ed. (New York: Harper
      and Row, n.d.).
27   Hans Hofmann, *Search for the Real*, ed. Sara T. Weeks and Bartlett H.
      Hayes, Jr., (Cambridge: M.I.T. Press, 1967), p. 43.
28   Ibid., p. 44.
29   This idea reminds us of the method of geometric analysis developed by
      Alfred North Whitehead, which he called extensive abstraction. Accord-
      ing to Whitehead's approach, we begin with regions of physical space and
      abstract geometric forms from them. Thus, we might think of a point as
      the limit of a series of smaller and smaller regions that we abstract from
      physical space.
30   Gombrich, *Art and Illusion*, p. 373.

CHAPTER FOUR   THE ARTIST AND THE VISIBLE WORLD

1   See especially the following sources: Merleau-Ponty, "Indirect Language
      and the Voices of Silence", *Signs*, pp. 39-83; "Eye and Mind", *The Primacy
      of Perception*, pp. 159-190; and *The Visible and the Invisible*, ed. Claude Lefort
      and trans. Alphonso Lingis (Evanston, Ill.: Northwestern University,
      1968).
2   Merleau-Ponty, *Signs*, p. 46.
3   Merleau-Ponty, *Signs*, p. 43.
4   Merleau-Ponty discusses the diacritical theory of language in *Signs* pp.
      39ff. See Ferdinand de Saussure, *Course in General Linguistics*, ed. Charles
      Bally, Albert Sechehaye, and Albert Riedlinger, trans. Wade Baskin (New
      York: Philosophical Library, 1959).
5   A similar idea is to be found in Wilfrid Sellars' discussion of the
      derivation of distinctions from language. He notes for example that "one
      can have the concept of green only by having a whole battery of concepts
      of which it is one element." He says this in the context of arguing that
      'looks green' is derivative from things 'being green', and the latter
      depends on our mastery of a whole battery of color concepts. See Wilfrid
      Sellars, "Empiricism and the Philosophy of Mind", *Science, Perception and
      Reality*, (New York: Routledge and Kegan Paul, 1963), pp. 147-148.
6   Merleau-Ponty, *Signs*, p. 41.
7   Ibid.
8   See Sellars, *Science, Perception and Reality*, especially pp. 173ff.
9   Merleau-Ponty, *The Visible and the Invisible*, p. 155.
10   Merleau-Ponty, *Signs*, p. 47.
11   Merleau-Ponty, "An Unpublished Text: A Prospectus of His Work,"
      trans. Arleen B. Dallery, *The Primacy of Perception*, p. 5.

12   Merleau-Ponty, *Signs*, p. 48.
13   Merleau-Ponty, *The Primacy of Perception*, p. 162.
14   Merleau-Ponty's term for man's relationship to the visible world is that
        man is an *exemplar sensible*. For discussion of this concept see *The Visible and
        the Invisible*, pp. 135ff.
15   Concerning this point, Merleau-Ponty quotes Andre Marchand as
        follows: "In a forest, I have felt many times over that it was not I who
        looked at the forest. Some days I felt that the trees were looking at me,
        were speaking to me . . . . I was there, listening . . . . I think that the
        painter must be penetrated by the universe and not want to penetrate
        it. . . . " *Primacy of Perception*, p. 167.
16   Merleau-Ponty, "Cezanne's Doubt," *Sense and Non-Sense*, p. 17.
17   Merleau-Ponty observes: "Personal life, expression, understanding, and
        history advance obliquely and not straight toward ends or concepts. What
        one too deliberately seeks he does not find; and he who on the contrary
        has in his meditative life known how to tap its spontaneous source never
        lacks for ideas or values." *Signs*, p. 83.
18   Merleau-Ponty, *Sense and Non-Sense*, p. 17.
19   Ibid.
20   Pierre Bourdieu, *Outline of a Theory of Practice*, trans. Richard Nice.
        (Cambridge: Cambridge University Press, 1977), p. 15.
21   Merleau-Ponty, *The Primacy of Perception*, p. 162.
22   See especially Merleau-Ponty's discussion in Chapter IV, "The Inter-
        twining—The Chiasm", *The Visible and the Invisible*, pp. 130-155.
23   Merleau-Ponty, *Signs*, pp. 58-59.
24   James J. Gibson, *The Ecological Approach to Visual Perception*. (Boston:
        Houghton Mifflin Co., 1979).
25   Ibid., p. 43.
26   Ibid., p. 61.
27   Ibid., p. 57.
28   Ibid. See particularly pp. 73ff.
29   Ibid., pp. 22 and 35.
30   Ibid., p. 15.
31   Ibid., pp. 18-19.
32   Merleau-Ponty, *The Visible and the Invisible*, pp. 135ff.
33   Ibid., p. 131.
34   Gibson, *The Ecological Approach to Visual Perception*, p. 283.
35   Ibid., p. 284.
36   John F. A. Taylor, *Design and Expression in the Visual Arts*, (New York: Dover,
        1964), pp. 221-222.
37   Merleau-Ponty writes, "For painters the world will always be yet to be
        painted, even if it lasts a million years. . . it will end without having been
        conquered in painting." *Primacy of Perception*, p. 189.
38   Ibid., p. 165.

39   For discussion of this subject see Merleau-Ponty "Eye and Mind", *The Primacy of Perception*, pp. 169ff. The discussion by both Whitehead and Merleau-Ponty of the abstractness of the scientific account of bodies reminds the author of a striking passage in Spinoza, where he argues that a more adequate concept of bodies is needed. He says: "But my opponents will say, that from the laws of nature alone, insofar as it is considered to be corporeal merely, it cannot be that the causes of architecture, painting, and things of this sort, which are the results of human art alone, could be deduced, and that the human body, unless it were determined and guided by the mind, would not be able to build a temple. I have already shown however, that they do not know what the body can do, nor what can be deduced from a consideration of its nature alone...." Benedict Spinoza,(Part III, Scholium to Proposition II), *Ethics*, trans. W.H. White, in *Spinoza Selections*, ed. John Wild (Scribner, 1930), p. 211.

40   Merleau-Ponty, *Signs*, p. 67.

41   Merleau-Ponty, *The Primacy of Perception*, p. 181.

CHAPTER FIVE   MEANING AND CULTURAL REGULARITIES

1   Alfred Barr indicates that Pierre Matisse attributed the painting's inspiration to a dance (the *farandole*) which he saw in a popular dance hall. See Alfred H. Barr, Jr., *Matisse, His Art and His Public*, (New York: Museum of Modern Art, 1951), p. 135. Other interpreters attribute it to the Catalan dance-in-the-round, known as the *sardana*, which Matisse had seen in southern France. See John Russell, *The World of Matisse*, (New York: Time-Life Series, 1969), p. 88.

2   Hans Georg Gadamer, "The Universality of the Hermeneutic Problem", *Philosophical Hermeneutics*, trans. and ed. by David E. Linge, (Berkeley: University of California Press, 1976), p. 7.

3   In formulating the account of visual culture in this way, I am following the practice followed by Joseph Margolis. See two of his works for extended discussion of this theme: *Art and Philosophy*, (Atlantic Highlands, N.J.: Humanities Press, 1980); and *Culture and Cultural Entities*, (Boston: D. Reidel, 1984).

4   Margolis, *Culture and Cultural Entities*, p. 11.

5   Ibid., pp. 11-12. For a discussion of the distinction between inten*t*ional and intensional see Chapter I in Margolis.

6   Margolis discusses this distinction between token and type and its implications for understanding culture in several places. Most recently in *Culture and Cultural Entities*, pp. 13ff. Margolis treats the type-token feature as an essential feature of cultural entities.

7   Roman Jakobson, *Six Lectures on Sound and Meaning*, trans. John Meapham. (Cambridge: M.I.T. Press, 1981). See Lecture I for discussion of these distinctions.

8   Ibid., pp. 10-11.

9   Ibid., pp. 26-27.

10   Ibid., pp. 62-63. Jakobson emphatically insists on the negative value of phonemes. "Whereas all other elements have specific, positive content, direct meaning, phonemes by contrast have a solely differential value, thus a purely negative value." Ibid., p. 63.

11   Ibid., p. 52.

12   Clifford Geertz, *The Interpretation of Cultures*, (New York: Basic Books, 1973), p. 37.

13   Ibid., p. 43.

14   Ibid., p. 5.

15   Jakobson, *Six Lectures on Sound and Meaning*, p. 81.

16   Ibid., p. 86.

17   John Dewey, *Art as Experience*, (New York: Minton, Balch and Co., 1934), p. 287.

18   Ibid., pp. 195-196.

19   Ibid., p. 200.

20   For a view of musical meaning similar to the one developed in this chapter see Jacques Barzun, "The Meaning of Meaning in Music: Berlioz Once More," *The Musical Quarterly*, (Vol. LXVI, January, 1980), pp. 1-20.

21   Nietzche, *The Birth of Tragedy*, p. 102.

22   Langer, *Feeling and Form*, p. 27.

23   Dewey, *Art as Experience*, p. 238.

24   Ibid., p. 239.

25   Margolis, *Culture and Culture Entities*, p. 11. Quoted above, p. 113.

26   Bourdieu, *Outline of a Theory of Practice*, p. 72.

27   Gadamer, *Truth and Method*, p. 93.

28   Ibid., p. 98.

29   Ibid., p. 92.

30   Bourdieu, *Outline of a Theory of Practice*, p. 21.

31   For discussion of this topic see Bourdieu's "Generative Schemes and Practical Logic: Invention Within Limits", *Outline of a Theory of Practice*, Chap. 3.

32   Ibid., p. 110.

33   Ibid., p. 113.

34   Ibid., p. 9.

35   Ibid., p. 87.

36   Ibid., p.88. Bourdieu argues that the Kabyle child masters a wide range of his culture from observing adult behavior. See pp. 15ff for his discussion of the sense of honor.

37   Geertz, *The Interpretation of Cultures*, p. 47.

38   For a discussion of this distinction, see John Dewey, *Art as Experience*, pp. 60ff.

39   Ibid., p. 64.
40   Merleau-Ponty, *The Visible and the Invisible*, p. 155.

CHAPTER SIX

1   Clifford Geertz, *The Intepretation of Cultures*, p. 5.
2   Ibid., p. 26.
3   Ibid., p. 13.
4   A noteworthy example of this is found in Norwood Russell Hanson's discussion of causality in Chapter III of *Patterns of Discovery*, (Cambridge: Cambridge University Press, 1965). Hanson contrasts mechanical accounts of causality, which treat causes and effects as links in a chain, with a view of causality utilizing more general concepts to explain less general ones, or which explain events or sets of conditions. For example, Hanson argues that the explanatory levels move upward with the diagnosis that a mark on the arm is a *scar*, and that this general type of feature is explainable from the inflicting of a *wound*. 'Wound' here is more general than 'scar'; and the causal explanation in this case is to be distinguished from one which attributes the scar to a surgeon's knife, since we do not say that surgeon's wound their patients. See especially, p. 56 for a discussion of causal explanation that comes close to token-type analysis.
5   John Dewey, *Theory of Valuation, International Encyclopedia of Unified Science*, Vol 2, No. 4, (Chicago: University of Chicago Press, 1959), pp. 9-12.
6   Dewey, *Art as Experience*, p. 48.
7   Dewey, *Theory of Valuation*, pp. 40-43.
8   Ibid., p. 60.
9   Dewey, *Art as Experience*, p. 54.
10   Ibid., p. 259.
11   See, for example, Dewey's discussion of artistic media and language in *Art As Experience*, pp. 106ff. See also p. 287 for another example.
12   Gadamer, *Truth and Method*, p. 93.
13   Ibid., pp. 99ff.
14   Ibid., p. 94.
15   Ibid.
16   See Chapters VII and VIII of Dewey's *Art As Experience* for a discussion of this topic.
17   Ibid., p. 99.
18   Ibid., p. 126.
19   Paul Ricoeur, *Interpretation Theory*, (Fort Worth, Texas: Texas Christian University, 1976), pp. 40-41.
20   Merleau-Ponty, *Signs*, p. 56.

21   Gadamer, *Truth and Method*, p. 98.
22   This was quoted on p. 127.
23   The reader should note the contrast between equivalence in practice and Gombrich's idea of visual equivalents for objects.
24   For an excellent analysis of complex time factors see Clifford Geertz's "Person, Time and Conduct in Bali," *Interpretation of Cultures*, pp. 360-411.
25   Jakobson, *Six Lectures on Sound and Meaning*, pp. 98ff.
26   Ibid., pp. 100-103.
27   Ibid., p. 106.
28   Ricoeur, *Interpretation Theory*. See Chapter III, especially pp. 50ff.
29   Ibid., p. 52.
30   Nelson Goodman, *The Languages of Art*, p. 85.
31   Ibid., p. 93.
32   Ricoeur, *Interpretation Theory*, pp. 52-53.
33   Merleau-Ponty, *The Primacy of Perception*, p. 40. Ricoeur states a similar idea when he says: "Thanks to writing, man and only man has a world and not just a situation. . . . " *Interpretation Theory*, p. 36.
34   Ricoeur, *Interpretation Theory*, p. 37.
35   Gadamer, *Truth and Method*, pp. 112-113.
36   Dewey, *Theory of Valuation*, p. 66.
37   The difference between Gadamer's concept and Dewey's is evident in the following passage from Dewey: "When things which exist around us, which we touch, see, hear, and taste are regarded as interrogations for which an answer must be sought (and must be sought by means of deliberate introduction of changes till they are reshaped into something different), nature as it already exists ceases to be something which must be accepted and submitted to, endured or enjoyed, just as it is. It is now something to be modified, to be intentionally controlled . . . . Nature as it it exists at any particular time is a challenge, rather than a completion . . . . " *The Quest for Certainity: A Study of the Relation of Knowledge and Action.* (New York: Minton, Balch, and Co., 1934), p. 100.
38   Gadamer, *Truth and Method*, p. 102.
39   Gablik, *Progress in Art*, pp. 40-41.
40   The perceptive reader will not be surprised to find Dewey saying something strikingly similar. He writes, "Industry displaces magic, and science reduces myth, when the elements that enter into the constitution of the consummatory whole are discriminated, and each one has its own particular place in sequential order assigned to it. . . . " John Dewey, *Experience and Nature*, (Chicago: Open Court, 1926), p. 387.

Chapter Seven   Creavity and Truth

1   Merleau-Ponty, *Signs*, p. 109. My italics.

2   Ricoeur, *Interpretation Theory*, p. 36.
3   For a full discussion of the notion of "rightness of rendering" see Nelson
     Goodman, *Ways of Worldmaking*, Chapter VII. In contrast with the view I
     am presenting, Goodman restricts the concept to truth to cases of
     objective validation. He applies notions of *fit* to art works, instead of
     notions of truth.
4   Heidegger, *Poetry, Language, Thought*, pp. 41-42.
5   Richard Rorty, "The World Well Lost," *The Journal of Philosophy*, 69 (1972),
     p. 662. Reprinted in Richard Rorty, *Consequences of Pragmatism*. (Minnea-
     polis: University of Minnesota, 1982), p. 14.
6   Merleau-Ponty, *Signs*, p. 52.
7   Ibid., p. 69.
8   Ibid., p. 68.
9   Ibid., p. 68.
10   Ibid., p. 60.
11   Nietzsche, *Twilight of the Idols*, p. 86.
12   Gadamer, *Truth and Method*, pp. 264-265.
13   Gadamer, *Philosophical Hermeneutics*, p. 16. Even more broadly, Gadamer
     provides a positive account of prejudices, defined by him as "biases of
     our openness to the world. They are simply conditions whereby we
     experience something. . . . " Ibid., p. 9.
14   Again this contrasts with John Dewey, who says: "The moral function of
     art is to remove prejudice, do away with the scales that keep the eye from
     seeing, tear away the veils due to wont and custom, perfect the power to
     perceive." *Art As Experience*, p. 325.
15   Wittgenstein, *Zettel*, paragraph 231.
16   Ibid., paragraph 233.
17   Merleau-Ponty, *Sense and Non-Sense*, p. 11.
18   Nietzsche, *Twilight of the Idols*, p. 39.
19   Hofmann, *Search for the Real*, p. 61.
20   Merleau-Ponty, *Signs*, p. 120.

CHAPTER EIGHT   ART AND SELF-UNDERSTANDING

1   Gadamer, "Aesthetics and Hermeneutics," *Philosophical Hermeneutics*, p.
     95.
2   For a fuller discussion of these themes in Matisse, see Kate Linker,
     "Meditations on a Goldfish Bowl: Autonomy and Analogy in Matisse,"
     Artforum, 19 (1980), pp. 65-73.
3   Nietzsche, *Will to Power*, paragraph 507.
4   Gadamer, *Philosophical Hermeneutics*, p. 104. John Dewey also attributes
     moral significance to art. He cites Shelley's idea that "imagination is the
     great instrument of moral good. . . . " *Art As Experience*, p. 347. Dewey

agrees with Shelley, adding that the "moral prophets of humanity have always been poets. . . ." Ibid., p. 348.

5   Nietzsche, *The Will to Power*, paragraph 584.

6   Ibid., paragraph 552.

7   For discussion of this feature of Picasso's thought see Andre Malraux, *Picasso's Mask*, pp. 10-13.

8   Geertz, *The Interpretation of Cultures*, p. 129.

9   Nietzsche, *The Birth of Tragedy*, p. 52.

10   Gadamer, *Truth and Method*, p. 446.

11   Nietzsche, *Will to Power*, paragraph 809.

12   Merleau-Ponty, *Signs*, p. 74.

13   Ibid.

14   Friedrich Nietzsche, *The Case of Wagner*, trans. Walter Kaufmann. (New York: Random House, 1967), Section 8.

15   Merleau-Ponty, *Signs*, p. 52.

Index

Artist *(cont.)*
understanding, 4, 18; as willful, self-
conscious agent, 17, 38–39, 63, 140,
193n.3. *See also* Style
Authenticity, 164
Autonomy, 4, 73, 96

Barr, Alfred, Jr., 196n.10, 199n.1
Barzun, Jacques, 200n.20
Bathers (Cezanne): 59, 82, 101, 104, 135,
139, 173; *Figure 11* 61
Bernstein, Leonard, 56
Beliefs, 166–167
Beyond Good and Evil (Nietzsche), 194n.8
Birth of Tragedy, The (Nietzsche), 32, 63
Boccioni, Umberto: *Muscular Dynamism*,
107, 108, (fig. 20) 150
Body. *See* Embodiment
Bourdieu, Pierre: on cultivated
dispositions, 94; on cultural regularities,
124–127, 148–149; on honor, 136; on
the Kabyle 125, 136, 200n.36; on
strategies vs. rules, 127; on time, 127,
148
Britten, Benjamin, *Peter Grimes*, 34–35
Broadway Boogie Woogie (Mondrian): 102;
Figure 18 103
Brody, J.J., 196n.25

Causality: of art works, 3, 32, 62; cultural,
113, 129, 132–135, 169; vs. historical
sources, 136; vs. patterns, 149; and the
meaning of actions, 33, 46–47; and
temporal development, 148–149, 170,
195n.24; and token-type analysis,
201n.4
Cezanne, Paul: on abstract construction,
59, 62, 93; *Bathers*, 59, 61 (fig. 11), 82,
101, 104, 135, 139; on consciousness
and landscape, 91; *Landscape Near Aix*,
91–94, 92 (fig. 17), 101; on making
visible, 22, 24; on relationships on the
canvas, 77, 97–98; on repeated studies
(Mt. St. Victoire), 106, 173; on visual
types created by, 143–144
Chinese Landscape Painting, 74, 77
Clinical, analysis of culture, 134–136,
148–149, 170

Color: biological and cultural aspects of,
101, 114; in Cezanne, 93–94; Dewey
on, 120; diacritical interpretation of,
86–88, 100, 197n.5; generality and, 100;
in Hofmann, 77–80, 82; as invariant,
99–100; in Monet, 160; in Munch, 114;
in Rembrandt, 11
Concerning the Spiritual in Art (Kandinsky),
26
Condensed Image, 15–16, 37, 54, 146,
165, 193n.4
Consciousness: as counterpart of objects
89, 91, 141; and culture, 111, 127, 132;
and cultural regularities, 121, 131; and
individual control, 140, 170; and
narrative, 153; and self-presenation,
140–141; and time, 149, 153
Consistency-building, 56
Conventionalism, 5–6, 84, 106, 167
Correspondence: between pictures and
things, 2, 9, 11; theory of truth, 8, 11,
24
Course in General Linguistics (Saussure),
197n.4
Creative: act, 16, 17; process, 3, 16–17,
51, 90, 93, 120, 153, 193n.3
Creative Person: vs. the creative mind,
88–90, 157, 188; and culture, 110–112;
and embodiment, 96; and perception,
97; and token-type analysis, 141
Creativity: and the artist's values, 2; and
culture, 46, 63, 110; and historical
sources, 52, 56, 57; and innovation, 25;
semantical vs. psychological theory of,
112; and truth, 3, 23, 25, 157, 174; and
visual schemata, 58
Cubism, 58, 136, 177, 182
Cultivated Dispositions, 94–95, 110
Culture: and the artist, 18; barrier vs.
access, 157; and causality, 113, 129,
132–135, 169; clinical analysis of,
134–136, 148–149, 170; and color, 101,
114; as collective, 111; and the creative
person, 110–112; and creativity, 46, 63,
110; and expression, 46, 50, 91, 168;
the growth of, 43, 168; as language-like,
112, 140, 171, 199n.3; and linguistic
boundaries, 113–114, 125; and